Ireland's Most Wanted™

The Top 10 Book of Celtic Pride, Fantastic Folklore, and Oddities of the Emerald Isle

Brian M. Thomsen

Potomac Books, Inc.

WASHINGTON, D.C.

Library of Congress Cataloging-in-Publication Data
Thomsen, Brian.
  Ireland's most wanted : the top 10 book of Celtic pride, fantastic folklore, and oddities of the Emerald Isle / Brian M. Thomsen.— 1st ed.
        p. cm. — (Most wanted)
  Includes bibliographical references and index.
  ISBN 1-57488-727-0 (pbk. : alk. paper)
  1. Ireland—Miscellanea. 2. Curiosities and wonders—Ireland. I. Title. II. Series.

  DA906.T48 2005
  941.5—dc22

                                        2004024013

Printed in Canada on acid-free paper that meets the American National Standards Institute Z39-48 Standard.

Potomac Books, Inc.
22841 Quicksilver Drive
Dulles, Virginia 20166

First Edition

10   9   8   7   6   5   4   3   2   1

To all who have given their lives in the name of Irish nationalism.

To all who have shared the wonders of the Emerald Isle with the rest of the world.

To all who have had their efforts grievously overlooked by the rest of world (Gerry Adams).

. . . And to all the artists, writers, thespians, discoverers, etc., who hail from the old sod at some point in their ancestry.

. . . and, of course, God's greatest blessing on the Guinness family.

Long Live Ireland—One Nation, One Peace!

Contents

Photographs

Introduction

Irish is more than a nationality—it's a state of being.

What other cultural background allows you to demand a kiss, celebrate the wearing of a color (green), toast the wee folk, and take pride in one's ire and readiness to fight?

What other nationality is celebrated by parades and parties that allow even the nonblessed to declare themselves Irish for one day (even if your last name is Giuliani or Bloomberg)?

Irish is a culture of kings and rebels, saints and sprites, and warriors and wee folk, filled with bloody battles, adventurous epics, fabulous feats, and passionate politics.

From sports to poetry, and from rock 'n' roll to Wilde and Shaw, the Irish have left their mark on the world in accomplishments and competition, spirited and otherwise.

Who can forget the epic of the Ulster cycle or the dense majesty of *Finnegan's Wake* or the pennywhistle musical accents of the Corrs and the Pogues?

You don't have to be born of the old sod to love her music and prose.

And what of her exports . . . her fine linens and crystal, her spirited whiskeys and ales, and her eloquent sons and daughters always ready with a smile, a strong back, a keen wit, and a bit of blarney to make the world a better place? Names like Murphy, Kennedy, and Fitzpatrick have found their way into telephone directories around the world.

True, it is also a heritage of oppression and injustice filled with tyrants and monsters who dared to bend the virtuous Irish to their will only to be frustrated by their stouthearted resistance.

Not even the devilish, most monstrous, maleficent one, Oliver Cromwell, was able to crush her spirit, for Ireland and her people are forever, and all over, in books, and in movies, on television and in music.

Ireland's Most Wanted merely provides a peek at all things Irish, for a peek at the Irish is a panorama of any other culture.

Irish Emblems, Terms, and Things Known by All

What comes to mind when you hear the word, Ireland? Below are some things most commonly associated with the Emerald Isle.

1. **SHAMROCK**

A low-growing clover plant indigenous to Ireland alleged to have been used by St. Patrick as a metaphor for the Holy Trinity, this bit of Irish greenery has become the florist and card shop's equivalent of the Christmas season's mistletoe and poinsettias for the month of March.

2. **SHILLELAGH**

The shillelagh is an Irish cudgel fashioned from a bramble bough, thought to be wielded by leprechauns and Irish warriors (who supplemented its heft with the occasional addition of molten lead). Now it is primarily seen as a once-a-year walking stick for Hibernians and other St. Patrick's Day marchers.

3. POT OF GOLD

The treasure of the leprechauns is supposedly located at the end of the rainbow. Other legends think of the pot of gold as buried treasure, perhaps an allusion to wealth hidden from Anglo-oppressors. Most illustrations of the pot feature the gold as coins rather than nuggets.

4. CLADDAGH

A heart with a crown at the top and a pair of hands at either side makes up the claddagh. The heart represents love, the crown loyalty, and the hands friendship.

This, too, has become a greeting card staple with increased sales in the first quarter of the year, as it is equally exploitable for Valentine's and St. Patrick's Day promotions.

5. ERIN GO BRAGH

Quite simply, "Ireland for ever," one sees "erin go bragh" emblazoned on streamers, cardboard, and anywhere Irish revelers (or those who just wish to pass themselves off as such) gather.

6. SINN FEIN

Literally "ourselves alone," this is the name of the Irish Republican Army's (IRA's) political wing and the spearhead of the Irish Nationalist movement since the days of the Rising.

7. BODHRAN

A traditional Irish drum, sort of a Celtic equivalent of the Indian tom-tom, the bodhran can provide a marching beat or can accompany pennywhistle tunes.

8. BLACK 47

This is a reference to the worst year of the Great Famine in Ireland when landowners maintained foreign export of grain and potato products while indigenous farmers starved. Nowadays, it serves as a moniker for music bands and mixed drinks.

9. SHANTY IRISH

Derogatory term for Irish peasantry and poor, shanty Irish is the Emerald Isle equivalent of trailer trash.

10. LACE CURTAIN IRISH

Not to be outdone, this is a derogatory term for Irish genteel class, the old sod equivalent of Park Avenue swells.

Proverbs and Maxims

The Irish are known for their sayings almost as much as Confucius is. Below are some of the best.

1. CONSCIENTIOUS WORK

You'll never plow a field by turning it over in your mind.

2. A WELL-ROUNDED EDUCATION

Better knowledge of evil than evil without knowledge.

3. ACTS OF CHRISTIAN CHARITY

A little help is better than a lot of pity.

4. SINCERITY AND FIDELITY

Promising but not fulfilling is worse than refusing.

5. MATURITY AND PERSPECTIVE

Young people don't know what age is, and old people forget what youth was.

6. RISKS OF AMBITION

The doorstep of a great house is slippery.

7. TRUE FRIENDSHIP

A friend that can be bought is not worth buying.

8. IMPORTANCE OF THE WRITTEN WORD

A scholar's ink lasts longer than a martyr's blood.

9. THE SEXES

There are three types of men who fail to understand women—young men, old men, and middle-aged men.

10. DOWNSIDE OF SPIRITED DRINKS

Drink is the curse of the land. It makes you fight with your neighbor, it makes you shoot at your landlord—and it makes you miss.

Saintly Scions

The religious heritage of the Emerald Isle is an unusual amalgam of Catholics and Celts that has produced an uncomfortable mixture of folklore and faith, but on the plus side of pragmatism, missionaries begat monasteries that mentored and preserved learning. With so much of benefit to the Irish people derived from these early holy individuals, it is a tragedy that political strife led to an even wider divide between church and state in Ireland than in other, more secular nations.

1. ST. PATRICK

Patron saint of Ireland, born 389 and died 461, this most famous of all Irishmen (let alone Irish saints) was actually born in Britain, the son of a Roman official, named Calpurnius. As the story goes he was kidnapped by pirates and sold into slavery in County Mayo, where he endured the yoke of oppression for six years before finally escaping back to Scotland and entering monastic life. Moving up through the ranks of the British church, he eventually was ordained a missionary bishop to Ireland, where he preached conversion in the northern and western parts of the Emerald Isle.

Much of what we know of him is derived from two works he authored, "The Confessions" and "Letter to Coroticus." The stories of his divine dream visitations, his banishment of snakes, and his use of the shamrock to illustrate the concept of the holy trinity are, unfortunately, all apocryphal.

2. ST. BRIGID

Very few facts are actually known about St. Brigid, even though she is the second most prominent Irish saint after St. Patrick. Indeed, some contemporary scholars view her as an opportunistic co-option of the pagan Celtic goddess, Brid.

That said, St. Brigid is credited with establishing a women's monastery at Kildare in 500 and serving as its first abbess.

She has been called Mary of the Gaels, and it is widely believed that medieval Knights of Chivalry claimed her as their patron saint and, indeed, addressed their wives as "brides" in her honor.

Cogitosus's *Life of Brigid* is primarily a collection of myths and legends connected to her alleged miracles and should not be viewed as an authorized biography.

3. ST. FINIAN

Born in County Meath at the end of the fifth century, St. Finian is regarded as the patriarch of the Irish monastic movement. He believed that the ascetic life was the best way to live God's wishes, which was in stark contrast to the decadent and cushy lives of the Catholic bishops of the time.

He established a monastic school at Clonard that was considered the most famous one of its time, and his most dedicated disciples, who established monasteries of their own, became known as the twelve apostles of Ireland.

St. Finian died of plague in 549.

4. ST. BRENDAN

Born and baptized in County Kerry, St. Brendan established numerous monasteries throughout Ireland, including one at Galway that became one of the safe houses for civilization during the time when the Irish were civilization's custodian.

In addition to his holy works, St. Brendan is known as the Navigator, having traveled extensively with exploits as recorded in an ancient manuscript, *The Navigatio Sancti Brendani,* which includes an account of his meeting with St. Patrick and Judas Iscariot (temporarily released from Hell). Despite these bits of fancy, a recent group of explorers has charted the course of his journey and has even duplicated it using the available technology of Brendan's time, though the travelers observed no damned or divine beings along the way.

5. ST. OLIVER PLUNKETT

Born in Country Meath in 1629, Plunkett entered the priesthood and spent most of his tenure in Rome, until he was appointed archbishop of Armagh in 1669.

He immediately took it upon himself to foster better relationships with the crown and local government, but, unfortunately, he was wrongfully implicated in the so-called Popish plot to assassinate Charles II. As a result he was hanged, drawn, and quartered, along with the other alleged conspirators.

He was canonized in 1975.

6. ST. CIARAN

Considered the firstborn of all Irish saints—yes, even before St. Patrick—St. Ciaran studied on the Continent before returning to Ireland, where he preached the word of God.

He is widely associated with an affinity for animals and miraculously restoring life to the dead as well as the usual lackluster accomplishments of establishing a monastery and a convent and the religious orders that resided therein.

7. ST. COLUMBA OF IONA

Born of royal blood in Donegal in 521, St. Columba studied under St. Finian and was a leading Irish Catholic missionary among the barbarians of England and Scotland.

Several of his accomplishments have been embellished to the point of mytholgizing, including his alleged condemnation of a murderer at his victim's funeral, which resulted in the culprit dying on the spot and supposedly entering Hell as his victim entered heaven. St. Columba is also alleged to have instigated numerous tribal wars in the name of righteousness.

8. ST. ITA OF KILLEEDY

Born and christened Deidre in Waterford in 480, this saint took the name, Ita, when she entered the convent, having avoided marriage through the intercession of an angel. She established her own community of nuns in Limerick and preached the values of true faith, simplicity, and generosity.

9. ST. FIACRE OF MEAUX

Though primarily regarded as a French saint, St. Fiacre was actually born on the Emerald Isle. He established a hermitage at Meaux in 626 and is credited with numerous miraculous cures and providing hospice and refuge for many Irish pilgrims.

On a less sanctified note, a curved stone on which he used to sit on the hermitage grounds is widely considered to cure the hemorrhoids of those who sit on it.

10. ST. COMGALL OF BANGOR

Born in 516 in Dalriada, St. Comgall studied under St. Finian and founded a monastery at Bangor, where he preached austerity, discipline, and abstinence. In addition to miracles of mercy such as supernatural cures and gifts to the poor, he is credited with an equal number of acts of mystical vengeance against the less than charitable or dishonest, including striking a group of thieves blind for stealing vegetables from the monastery garden.

High Crosses

Given the huge role religion has played in the history of the Emerald Isle, it's not surprising that many overt symbols of the Church dot the Irish landscape. High crosses are one such symbol.

A high cross is an intricately carved, tall cross of stone typically containing a circle around its center. Most of these were carved between the eighth and twelfth century, and though many exist elsewhere, there is no doubt of the significance of the art form in the history of Ireland.

The following is a locale list for several major high crosses in the Irish countryside, each individually exquisite in its own right.

1. AHENNY CROSS

Located in County Tipperary, Ahenny boasts two ornate crosses: an east cross and a west cross, measuring 4.2 meters tall and 2.4 meters wide. Both are slightly damaged, although in different places, so when viewing both you can see what is missing where.

Their beauty remains, however, both have intricate interwoven designs carved all over.

2. CROSS AT MOONE

County Kildare is home to the Cross at Moone, which, at seventeen feet tall, is the second-tallest high cross in the country. Located in an old graveyard at an early Columban monastery, the cross was lost for centuries, its pieces broken and buried, before being reassembled in 1893. Carvings at the base depict such scenes as the miracle of the loaves and fishes, the temptation of St. Anthony, and the flight into Egypt.

3. MUIREDACH'S CROSS

Muiredach's Cross is the most famous of three high crosses in a churchyard in County Louth. This cross is believed to have been erected in honor of Muiredach, a cleric and former abbot who died in 922, based on a prayer for him carved into one side. Thus, most experts date the creation of the cross to the tenth century.

4. CROSS AT DYSERT O'DEA

County Clare's Cross at Dysert O'Dea is highlighted by a crucifixion figure with a bishop below. While many high crosses depict a ring surrounding the center, this one does not. Other carvings on the base include Adam and Eve and Daniel in the lion's den.

5. SOUTH CROSS AT KELLS

The South Cross at Kells, north of Boyne in County Meath in eastern Ireland, is one of the best preserved of the ninth-century crosses. The base depicts a carved scene of horsemen and soldiers. Kells is also home to a ruined cross, just the shaft of which remains.

6. HIGH CROSS AT CASTLEDERMOT

Castledermot in South Kildare is home to a monastery founded by St. Dermot (hence the name). There are two high crosses located here, plus the base of a third. The North Cross contains carvings of David with a harp, the sacrifice of Isaac, and the twelve apostles; the South Cross contains wonderfully decorative panels and other biblical carvings.

7. HIGH CROSS AT CLONMACNOISE

The High Cross at Clonmacnoise, in County Offaly, was erected over the grave of King Flann Sinna, who died in 914. Also called the Cross of Scriptures or King Flann's Cross, it contains panels depicting the life of St. Patrick. The original cross is housed in a museum, but a copy stands on the original site.

8. ST. PATRICK'S CROSS

St. Patrick's Cross, in Cashel, County Tipperary, is made of sandstone and is unique in that the arms of the cross are supported by columns to the ground, rather than by a ring surrounding the center of the cross as with most High Crosses. Resting now in the Hall of the Vicars, the cross was originally placed at a site where St. Patrick supposedly planted his staff.

9. CELTIC CROSS OF INISHMORE

The Aran Islands consist of three islands: Inishmore (or big island), Inishmaan (or middle island), and

Inisheer (or island to the east). Big island is perhaps a misnomer, or at least relatively so, as the island totals roughly sixteen square miles. Standing before a pub on Inishmore, though, is a Celtic cross. According to legend, the cross is encircled because St. Patrick noticed the locals worshipping the sun; when he converted them to Christianity he merged the recognized circular symbol of the sun with that of a cross.

10. CROSS OF CONG

Originally from County Mayo, the Cross of Cong is now located in the National Museum in Dublin. Unlike others on this list, the Cross of Cong is relatively small, roughly thirty inches tall. However, it is recognized as one of the finest works of art from twelfth-century Europe. It is decorated with silver, bronze, and precious stones, and at the center of the cross is a crystal that originally contained what is believed to have been a piece of the "true cross" on which Jesus was crucified.

Sites of Beauty and Wonder

Even without taking their history into account, these places, with their scenic views and mysterious formations, are beautiful and awe inspiring.

1. RING OF KERRY

The Ring of Kerry is a 110-mile route along the Iveragh Peninsula. It is traditionally toured counterclockwise, starting in Killarney and circling around to the picturesque town of Kenmare.

2. PURPLE CLIFFS OF MOHER

Located in County Clare, and rising more than seven hundred feet above the Atlantic waves crashing below, the top of the Cliffs of Moher afford you a view of the entire Clare coast, the Aran Islands, and—on a clear day—County Kerry and Connemara. On a sunny day the cliffs take on a purple hue, thus their name.

3. GIANT'S CAUSEWAY

Located in Bushmills, this is a three-mile stretch of roughly forty thousand tightly packed basalt rock columns (up to forty feet tall) that mysteriously jut up from the foot of a cliff and eventually disappear at sea. Supposedly this was built by the legendary hero, Finn MacCool.

4. HILL OF TARA

Located in County Meath, this Stonehenge-like round stone structure was believed to be the former seat of the High Kings and the capital of Celtic Ireland. Legend also had it that the Ark of the Covenant was buried there, a theory discounted by subsequent authorities in the vein of Indiana Jones.

5. PEAT BOGS

These wetlands, which used to cover 20 percent of all of Ireland, were formed from the slow accumulation of mosses over the years over a basis of decayed plants and other formerly living material. The resulting turf was used for fuel when burnt.

The Bog of Allen (370 square miles in counties Offaly, Laois, and Kildare) is a sight, but other scenic bogs are located in Shannonbridge, County Galway, and County Mayo.

It is useful to remember that the Emerald Isle is topographically a saucer-like bowl that has been filled in since the ice age, and a preponderance of the filler is peat. No matter, it makes for a beautiful countryside.

6. ORATORY OF GALARUS

A dry stone beehive-like structure located on the Dingle Peninsula, the Oratory of Gallarus is a tiny, perfectly preserved place of contemplation built of unmortared stone dating back to the ninth century.

7. DROMBERG STONE CIRCLE

Between Glandore and Rosscarbery in County Kinsale is the Dromberg Stone Circle, which dates back to the early Bronze Age. Charred bones were unearthed in the middle of the stone circle, and nearby there is evidence of a cooking trough of a perhaps sinister nature.

8. NEWGRANGE TUMULUS

Located in County Meath, Newgrange Tumulus is a mystifyingly awe-inspiring mound of more than two hundred thousand tons of earth and rock that a house a burial chamber thought to be over five thousand years old.

9. MITCHELSTOWN CAVES

Located in Burncourt, these caves are believed to be the largest system of river-transformed, limestone caverns in all of Ireland. The caves served as a hiding place for the Earl of Desmond in the sixteenth century and are noteworthy as the home of the very rare spider, *Porrhoma rosenhaueri*.

10. CROAGH PATRICK

In Murrisk, County Mayo, this twenty-five hundred-foot mountain has long been the site of St. Patrick pilgrimages, but the view is wonderful, too.

Irish Castles

Castles are an integral element of the Irish landscape, from the inner-city fortresses in town centers to the fortified country estates of less cosmopolitan clans and warlords. Depending on whom you talk to, either all of them are haunted or none of them is.

Nonetheless, they are well fortified, defended, and full of traps, even if some of them are of the tourist variety.

1. DUBLIN CASTLE

Located at Cork Hill off Dame Street in the city of Dublin, Dublin Castle is probably the most famous of all Irish castles because it was once the seat of English government in Ireland, despite the fact that it looks more like an armory than a castle. It was also the home of the Irish Crown Jewels until they mysteriously went missing a century ago.

The statue of Justice in the courtyard faces away from the city, which Dubliners have always felt was the case when justice was being dispensed by the English crown.

2. BLARNEY CASTLE

Located off the N20 outside of Cork City in County Cork, Blarney Castle is home to the world famous Blarney Stone. It was the seat of Munster province and has some of the most heavily fortified walls of any castle in Ireland—eighteen feet thick in parts, impressive even by seventeenth-century standards.

Attracting the tourist trade has undercut some of the castle's historical authenticity; addition of various enchanted attractions include a witch's kitchen and a leprechaun's tunnel.

3. DONEGAL CASTLE

Located at Donegal City Centre on the River Eske, Donegal Castle was built in the fifteenth century by an O'Donnell clan chieftain. Today there is ample evidence of seventeenth-century modifications and continental-influenced redecorating of the structure, from added wings to French tapestries.

4. KNAPPOGUE CASTLE

Located in County Clare just off the Ennis-Kilmurry road, southeast from Ennis in Quinn, this fifteenth-century stronghold of the McNamaras was desecrated by the occupation of the devil Oliver Cromwell's troops in the seventeenth century.

5. KILKENNY CASTLE

Located on The Parade in Kilkenny Town, County Kilkenny, this twelfth-century bastion is one of the more scenic castles in Ireland as it is surrounded by beautifully sculpted and tended gardens, including a formal rose garden on the shore of the River Nore.

6. LIMERICK CASTLE (ALSO KNOWN AS KING JOHN'S CASTLE)

Located on the banks of the River Shannon in Limerick on Nicholas Street, this formidable fortress

Limerick Castle, also known as King John's Castle.

was commissioned by King John in 1210 and is considered by many to be the best example of a fortified Norman structure on the Emerald Isle. The castle courtyard still displays many of the mechanisms of defense and offense from the time of its construction, including an authentic battering ram.

7. ROSS CASTLE (ALSO KNOWN AS CASTLE KILLARNEY)

South of the town of Killarney on Ross Road in County Kerry, this castle stronghold was the last holdout in the province of Munster to surrender to the insidious fiend, Oliver Cromwell, in 1652. Built in the 1400s by the O'Donoghue Ross clan, it is a classic central tower surrounded by a fortified wall with towers at the corners, as the Irish chieftains preferred.

8. DUNGUAIRE CASTLE

Located in Kinvara, in County Galway, Dunguaire is more of a museum attraction than a classic castle of the countryside. Supposedly it is built on the site of the palace of Guaire Aidhne, seventh-century king of Connaught, and has been fully restored, with each floor devoted to exhibitions depicting a different historical period.

9. MALAHIDE CASTLE

Located just outside of Dublin at Malahide, this castle was the family home of the Talbots, a distinguished, wealthy Irish clan, from 1185 to 1976. Still home to the family art collection, the castle is also the site of the last meal for fourteen members of the Talbot family on the eve of the Battle of the Boyne in 1690—by the following nightfall they were all dead.

10. **LISMORE CASTLE**

Located in County Waterford in Lismore above the River Blackwater, this scenic castle and estate was commissioned in the twelfth century. Sir Walter Raleigh owned it in the sixteenth century, though he never actually got to enjoy it or actually live there . . . a loss for tourists today as well since Lismore Castle is not open to the public.

Dublin History before 1850

Dublin, whose official Irish name is Bail Atha Cliath (the town of the ford of the hurdles), and whose Gaelic name is Dubh Linn (the dark pool), is located on the east coast of Ireland at the mouth of the River Liffey, facing the Irish Sea. It is the capital of the Emerald Isle, and its history is so rich it requires two different lists of top ten benchmarks.

1. **140 CE**

First official record of the settlement of Eblana, at the present site of Dublin, by Ptolemy in *Guide to Geography*.

2. **841 CE**

Vikings invade from the north and conquer a settlement, called Dubh Linn.

3. **1171**

The Normans seize Dublin but lose control of it to the English under Henry II, who makes it the center of English influence in Ireland.

4. **1204**

King John establishes Dublin Castle as the true stronghold of English rule in Ireland.

5. **1591–92**

Trinity College is established in Dublin with entry initially restricted to Anglicans. Future graduates will include Jonathan Swift, Edmund Burke, Wolfe Tone, and Samuel Beckett.

6. **1649**

Dublin surrenders to Oliver Cromwell, who uses Dublin Castle as the headquarters for his scourge of Ireland.

7. **1759**

The Golden Age of civilization in Ireland begins: the Guinness family opens a brewery in Dublin.

8. **1782**

The independent Irish parliament is established in Dublin and issues a Declaration of Independence proclaiming Ireland to be a nation unto itself.

9. **1803**

Independence uprising led by Robert Emmet attempts to seize Dublin Castle and fails; Emmet is executed in St. Catherine's Church.

DECLARATION OF INDEPENDENCE

WHEREAS the Irish people is by right a free people:

And whereas for seven hundred years the Irish people has never ceased to repudiate and has repeatedly protested in arms against foreign usurpation:

And whereas English rule in this country is, and always has been, based upon force and fraud and maintained by military occupation against the declared wish of the people:

And whereas the Irish Republic was proclaimed in Dublin on Easter Monday, 1916, by the Irish Republican Army, acting on behalf of the Irish people:

And whereas the Irish people is resolved to secure and maintain its complete independence in order to promote the common weal, to reestablish justice, to provide for future defence, to ensure peace at home and good will with all nations, and to constitute a national policy based upon the people's will, with equal right and equal opportunity for every citizen:

And whereas at the threshold of a new era in history the Irish electorate has in the General Election of December, 1918, seized the first occasion to declare by an overwhelming majority its firm allegiance to the Irish Republic:

Now, therefore, we the elected Representatives of the ancient Irish people in National Parliament assembled, do, in the name of the Irish nation, ratify the establishment of the Irish Republic and pledge ourselves and our people to make this declaration effective by every means at our command:

We ordain that the elected Representatives of the Irish people alone have power to make laws binding on the people of Ireland, and that the Irish Parliament is the only Parliament to which that people will give its allegiance:

We solemnly declare foreign government in Ireland to be an invasion of our national right which we will never tolerate, and we demand the evacuation of our country by the English Garrison:

We claim for our national independence the recognition and support of every free nation in the world, and we proclaim that independence to be a condition precedent to international peace hereafter:

In the name of the Irish people we humbly commit our destiny to Almighty God Who gave our fathers the courage and determination to persevere through long centuries of a ruthless tyranny, and strong in the justice of the cause which they have handed down to us, we ask His Divine blessing on this last stage of the struggle we have pledged ourselves to carry through to freedom.

Declaration of Independence

10. **1841**

Daniel O'Connell is elected the city's first Catholic mayor.

Modern Dublin History

1. **1853**

The Catholic University of Ireland is founded on St. Stephen's Green. Among its graduates are James Joyce and Eamon de Valera.

2. **1872**

Dublin's first tramline opens, linking the city with Rathmines.

3. **1904**

The Abbey Theatre is founded in Dublin, culminating in what is known as the Irish literary revival.

4. **1905**

Irish journalist Arthur Griffith founds Sinn Fein (Ourselves Alone) as the party of the republican political movement to campaign for Irish independence.

5. **1913**

The Dublin Lockout, during which more than twenty thousand laborers are barred from work by their employers for seeking trade union representation and negotiation rights.

6. **1916**

The Easter Rising, during which more than a thousand Irish nationalists seize the Dublin General Post Office.

7. **1921**

Dublin is named the capital of the new Irish Free State after signing of the Anglo-Irish Treaty.

8. **1980**

The first Anglo-Irish summit takes place in the city after the years of bombings, riots, and unrest since "Bloody Sunday" in 1972.

9. **1984**

The DART (Dublin Area Rapid Transit) opens between Bray and Howth with a spur to Maynooth, making Dublin truly a commuter city of the twentieth century.

10. **1991**

Dublin's urban rejuvenation results in the city being named a European City of Culture.

Irish Bars of Dublin

Bars in Ireland are more than just places to have a drink. They are public houses, or more succinctly, "pubs," rich with the legacy of their patrons and proprietors, past and present. And nowhere is that legacy richer than in the city of Dublin itself.

1. BALL O' MALT BAR

Located at Bow Street Distillery, Smithfield, the Irish Whiskey Corner is not really notable for its past as much as for its present, as it offers a tour and museum-like display of the history of distilling in Ireland, particularly as it pertains to Irish Whiskey. As part of the tour visitors are welcomed to the Ball o' Malt Bar, where they are encouraged to sample and snocker a wide variety of Irish whiskeys.

The combination of spirits and a spirited education is definitely a winning one.

2. BRAZEN HEAD

Located at 20 Lower Bridge Street, the Brazen Head is Dublin's oldest bar. Although it dates back to 1666, the structure itself—which earlier had been the Standfast Inn—was built in 1210. Not much has changed here since the years when Robert Emmet helped to plan the insurrection of 1803 on its premises.

3. THE BAILEY

Located at 2-3 Duke Street, the Bailey has been in business since 1837 and was a hangout of no less than Charles Parnell himself. A poets and writers' pub today, it is also the site of the door of 7 Eccles Street, the home of James Joyce's memorable protagonist from *Ulysses*, Leopold Bloom. The door was presented to the pub and publicly unveiled on June 16, 1967, by poet Patrick Kavanagh who had saved it from a renovator's axe.

In his day, Joyce was also a frequent customer . . . though unlike many writers hence, he never mentioned the establishment in his works.

4. TONER'S

Located at 139 Lower Baggot Street, Toner's has been in business for more than 175 years and still boasts such antiquities of the past as the original pump beer handles and numerous sundry drawers at the bar. Its greatest claim to fame, at least allegedly, is that it is the only Dublin pub in which William Butler Yeats ever had a drink—a sherry bought for him by Oliver St. John Gogarty. Once Yeats finished it he asked to be taken home, having sampled quite enough of the pub experience.

5. MULLINGAR HOUSE INN

Located at Chapelizod Bridge, Chapelizod, just south of Phoenix Park, Mullingar House Inn was established in 1694, primarily as a coach stop and inn for the stage from Mullingar.

The Inn is also significant for its Joycean heritage as noted on a commemorative plaque that reads "Home of all Characters and elements In James Joyce's novel *Finnegan's Wake*." The establishment had also been frequented by John Stanislaus Joyce (father of the author), who worked as secretary for a nearby distillery company from 1877 to 1880.

6. THE BLEEDING HORSE

Located at 25 Upper Camden Street, the Bleeding Horse was founded in 1649, and has been mentioned prominently in works by Joseph Sheridan LeFanu (author of the vampire classic, *Carmilla*), Sean O'Casey, and, of course, James Joyce.

7. KAVANAGH'S PUB

Located on Prospect Square, Glasnevin, Kavanagh's, also known as The Gravediggers' Pub, has been in the same family for more than eight generations, during which time it has pretty much remained the same from roof to original stone floor. It is also walking distance to the Glasnevin cemetery, perfect for a picnic.

8. GUINNESS HOP STORE

On Crane Street off James's Street, this is *the* place for Guinness at the place of its birth. Like the Ball o' Malt, there is a permanent exhibit on distilling and brewing with an obvious emphasis on the thick-brewed treasures of the Guinness empire.

9. NEARY'S

Located at 1 Chatham Street, right across from the actor's entrance for the Gaiety Theatre, Neary's has always been *the* actors' hangout in Dublin.

The neighborhood pub is of extreme social importance in Dublin.

10. DAVY BYRNES

Located at 21 Duke Street (across the street from the Bailey), this is still a prominent businessman's pub despite its literary legacy moniker from *Ulysses*: "He entered Davy Byrnes. Moral pub." The pub was established by its eponymous owner in 1873 and over the years has included among its clientele such prominent members of Sinn Fein as Michael Collins and Arthur Griffith and poets and playwrights such as Padraic O'Conaire and Brendan Behan (whose father-in-law painted a series of murals in the pub).

Irish Bars in New York City

As New York City is the home of the granddaddy of all St. Patrick's Day parades, it is safe to say that there will always be a little part of Ireland in that metropolis. And as a result there is also an abundance of New York Irish bars to rival Dublin.

Drinker beware, however: A name like "Blarney Stone," "Blarney Rock," or "Blarney Tavern" doesn't always assure the consumer of proper Irishness; sometimes it's just a franchise brand.

1. MCSORLEY'S OLD ALE HOUSE (15 EAST 7TH STREET)

The oldest licensed bar in Manhattan and, at 140, also the oldest Irish bar in the city . . . and still going strong, McSorley's is less a tourist attraction than an actual food and drink service tavern. It still accommodates a business and date crowd as well passionate imbibers from the Emerald Isle associated with the bar's cultural lineage.

2. RYAN'S DAUGHTER (350 EAST 85TH STREET)

As good an Irish bar as it is, Ryan's Daughter is a must for the soap opera set because it is clearly inspired by the bar of the same name in the long-running TV serial, *Ryan's Hope*. More than a TV tie-in, it's a good neighborhood watering hole.

3. TIR NA NOG (5 PENN PLAZA)

Taking its name from the Irish faerie realm, this midtown pub/restaurant offers a full Irish menu and a well-stocked bar of the Emerald Isle despite its location across from Madison Square Garden in the height of midtown. It's also a media hangout for the numerous communications workers of the neighborhood, including CNN and assorted business publications.

4. THE IRISH PUB (SEVENTH AVENUE AT 54TH STREET)

The Irish Pub is a bit noisy, but that's one of the drawbacks of its midtown locale. Not really a neighborhood hangout, the pub experiences crowds carefully timed to liquid lunches, after-work rendezvouses, and the post-theater nip rather than commuters.

5. FLANNERY'S BAR (205 WEST 14TH STREET)

Flannery's Bar boasts a fine set of ales and Irish entertainment from traditional and contemporary Irish music to step dancing. This establishment will satisfy the most demanding Celtic connoisseur as well as the casual tavern tippler.

6. ABBEY TAVERN (354 THIRD AVENUE AT 26TH STREET)

A neighborhood pub with a traditional menu of Irish fare, Abbey Tavern patrons are served by bartenders from the old sod . . . and the food and service are exemplary! Who can ask for more?

7. MCCORMACK'S PUB (365 THIRD AVENUE)

A fine place in Manhattan to get your fill of Irish sports from rugby to hurling, and the menu offers a full Irish breakfast, McCormack's features bartenders who know all the latest scores.

8. BROOKLYN

There is a great deal of turnover in the outer boroughs as neighborhoods trade ethnicities. These three Brooklyn bars all maintain their touch of the Irish: Kettle Black Bar and Restaurant; The Wicked Monk (with numerous appearances by garage bands and classic Irish groups like Black 47); and the Bean Post Inn of Bayridge, with plenty of Guinness on tap.

9. ROCKAWAY BEACH BARS

At one time this little community on a peninsula in Queens was known as Irish Town, with nary a block that didn't lay claim to a saloon operated by someone named Maguire, Healy, Curley, or Curran.

Those times have passed, but several of the local bars can trace their lineage to those days of green: Healy's Bar (10807 Rockaway Beach Drive), Blarney Castle (20224 Rockaway Point Boulevard), and the New Irish Circle (corner of 102nd Street and Rockaway Beach Boulevard). The New Irish used to be the Celtic crown of Irish pubs, but recent years have eroded its heritage with a "loud music" young people's crowd at night and automated off-track betting facilities during the day. Ah, for the days of the local Irish band and the neighborhood bookie.

10. SWIFT'S HIBERNIAN LOUNGE (34 EAST 4TH STREET)

An Irish bar homage to Dean Swift, including a pulpit from one of his parishes in Ireland, this tavern is a frequent hangout for English majors from nearby New York University. Less a rowdy pub than a literary saloon, it is still a paeon to its Irish heritage.

Irish Pub Drinks

The true native alcoholic Irish drink is poteen—Irish moonshine distilled from potatoes, barley, and yeast that has been made in Irish backwaters for more than four hundred years. Of course, making it is quite illegal, which does nothing to diminish its popularity. If you prefer to do your drinking in public, or rather, in a pub, there are many popular alternatives.

Note: Each entry is followed by a comment from Paddy the bartender, an authentic relic from the old sod.

1. IRISH COFFEE

Sweeten hot black coffee slightly with sugar, add a shot of Irish whiskey, and top with a shot of heavy cream deftly poured so it floats on top.

"The perfect little warm-me-up for when there's a bit of chill in the air. Old-timers like it and young folk too, seeing it as a perfect bridge between dinner and whatever young folks like to do late in the evening."

2. BLACK AND TAN

One-half ale, one-half Guinness stout.

"There's one thing I've never understood about the crowd that orders this. They think they're being prona-tionalist—don't they realize that the "black and tans" were the bad guys?"

3. LAGER AND BLACK

One-half lager, one-half Guinness stout.

"We used to just call it Guinness and beer—I guess this is what happens when those Carnaby Street PR folks get to make up the names."

4. STOUT AND BLACK

Guinness sweetened with blackcurrant syrup.

"The perfect drink for a manly man with a sweet tooth, and guaranteed to clear you out as well."

5. HOT WHISKEY PUNCH

Simmer boiled water with lemon, sugar, and cinna-mon, liberally mixed with room-temperature Irish whiskey.

"We used to call this Christmas punch. It was a nice little icebreaker at family get-togethers . . . until the fistfights broke out, of course."

6. BLACK VELVET

One-quarter Champagne, three-quarters Guinness stout.

"I've never seen a man order one of these . . . and the women who do would never be seen with the likes of me."

7. IRISH WHISKEY STRAIGHT UP

Irish whiskey by the shot.

"There's nothing like it in the world. In the old western movies this is what the real gunslingers drank. It's good for what ails you, no matter what the ailment might be."

8. IRISH BOILERMAKER

One shot of Irish whiskey in a mug of lager.

"For my money this is the perfect working man's drink. A shot downed to get you over the hurdle after a hard day's work with a beer chaser to savor and quench your thirst."

9. SHANDY

One-quarter lemon soda, three-quarters lager or ale.

"The perfect training drink for the youngsters . . . and not a bad thirst quencher for a summer's day either."

10. AND, OF COURSE, JUST PLAIN GUINNESS STOUT

A pint glass served at room temperature with just a touch of foamy head.

"Mother's milk—there's nothing like it in the world!"

Irish Cocktails

And then there are, of course, drinks that sound Irish but may or may not be "pub appropriate" depending on the clientele (ingredients are given in proportions rather than direct measures).

Paddy refused to comment on these; real Irish men don't waste the time to make these—it takes up otherwise valuable minutes that could be spent drinking.

1. EVERYBODY'S IRISH

One-half Irish whiskey, one-quarter green crème de menthe, one-quarter green chartreuse.

2. IRISH FLAG

Equal portions green crème de menthe, Bailey's Irish cream, and brandy, poured in liquid layers.

3. LEPRECHAUN MORNING

One-and-a-half parts Bailey's Irish Cream, one part Irish whiskey, three parts cold brewed coffee, with a splash of cherry brandy, served over crushed ice.

4. BANSHEE

One-and-a-half parts crème de bananas, one part white crème de cacao, one part light cream.

5. IRISH CANADIAN

One-half part Irish mist and one-and-a-half parts Canadian whiskey.

6. DIRTY LASS

One shot Bailey's Irish Cream, one shot vodka, one shot Kahlua, and a splash of green crème de menthe, served over ice.

7. BLACKPOOL TOWER

Two parts Bailey's Irish Cream, three-quarters part apricot brandy, a splash of gin, then mixed over ice and strained.

8. IRISH BAY HORSE

One-and-a-half parts Irish whiskey, one-half part Pernod, one-half part dark crème de cacao, one part heavy cream, sprinkle of nutmeg, then served over ice cubes with nutmeg sprinkled on top.

9. SCRUMPY STRONG

One part Irish whiskey and six parts hard cider, served over ice cubes.

10. HORSE FEATHERS OF THE OLD SOD

Two parts Irish whiskey to four parts ginger ale, with a dash of bitters, served over ice cubes.

Spirited Drinkers of the Old Sod

Let it not be said that the only spirits that bedevil the Irish are the wee folk. The caricature of the drunken Irishman is grossly exaggerated but, unfortunately, in concept not entirely dishonest. Some imbibe and embrace merriment, others melancholy. Some live from sweet dreams to stupor, while others are bedeviled in the nightmare of the drink.

Famous, fictional, and factually familiar, the old sod has more than its share of hard and fast drinkers who are ready to sing its praises and to rush out into the streets to defend the honor and freedoms of Ireland in a heated argument or a fistfight of the intoxicated.

1. PETER O'TOOLE

This fine and outstanding son of Ireland is legendary on both silver screen and stage for his masterful performances and his formidable alcoholic constitution. His performance in *My Favorite Year* was a marvelous blend of Errol Flynn and a jigger or two of O'Toole.

In numerous interviews concerning his Academy Award–nominated performance in *Lawrence of*

Arabia, O'Toole confided that camel riding was such a daunting activity it was better experienced drunk than sober so one doesn't have to focus as much on the sheer sense of terror one is experiencing.

Another famous exploit was from the memoirs of Michael Caine, who was doing London theater at the time O'Toole was being hailed as a talent to watch. One night their paths crossed in a hale-fellow-well-met manner that led to a pub crawl, resulting in both young thespians passing out in the flat of two young ladies. When Caine awoke he looked at O'Toole and inquired through his hangover, "What time is it?"

O'Toole replied, "You must be new at this. The correct question is, what day is it."

2. EUGENE O'NEILL

An award-winning Irish American playwright descended from Hugh "The Great" O'Neill, Second Earl of Tyrone, after thirty-seven years of excessive imbibing like his father before him, Eugene foreswore the bottle entirely (though it had already caused his health substantial detriment).

His greatest plays all include references to the drinking life: the family alcoholism/substance dependence in *A Long Day's Journey into Night* (a largely autobiographical work evolving around a family named Tyrone that is suspiciously reminiscent of the O'Neills), the bar denizens of *The Iceman Cometh*, and seduction through liquor in *A Moon for the Misbegotten*.

3. BRENDAN BEHAN

This patriot, poet, playwright, and all-around man of Irish literature loved liberty, life, and letters almost more than anything else. Unfortunately, one of things he did love more was "the drink."

Even when Behan gained prominence from his work, he was known to undercut his own credibility by drunken outbursts at readings, productions of his work, and media interviews.

He was still in his early forties when the drink took its toll, weakening Behan with diabetes and a heart condition. A memorable epitaph at the time of his death in 1964 summed it all up—"Too young to die, but too drunk to live."

4. RICHARD HARRIS

Another hard-working actor of the O'Toole era, Harris was once thought to be the silver-screen successor to Richard Burton (whom he succeeded in the role of Arthur in the film version of the Lerner and Lowe musical, *Camelot*).

After a few bit parts as miscellaneous drinking Irishman/RAF pilot/etc., Harris achieved leading man status and embraced the roaring boy lifestyle of whiskey, women, and "wow" with daring parts in films like *A Man Called Horse*.

Forswearing the bottle (which left his face weathered beyond its years) and reclaiming his faith, Harris returned to prominence toward the end of his career, while still maintaining the appearance of a man who embraced the glow of all things Irish, including its whiskey.

5. MALACHY MCCOURT

The alcoholic father of Pulitzer Prize–winning author Frank McCourt, he brought his American family back to Ireland during the 1930s, where they eked out a meager existence in the slums of Limerick.

It is McCourt's curse of the drink that condemns the family to an existence of poverty whence Frank must escape (which he did and later related in his acclaimed autobiographical works, *Angela's Ashes* and *'Tis*).

6. FRANCIS SYLVESTER MAHONY

Nineteenth-century humorist and "priest" of Cork who is mostly remembered for such poems as "The Bells of Shandon" and "The Lady of Lee," Mahony (also known as Father Prout) was a Jesuit in training at Clongowes Wood until he was kicked out after having been discovered taking young boys in his charge out to get drunk.

With the Jesuits no longer an option, Mahony first opted to be a secular priest and then withdrew from the clergy altogether to pursue his writing and the thirsty muse that inspired it.

7. GAINOR CHRIST

This Dublin bar patron provided the basis for the central character in J. P. Donleavy's *The Ginger Man*. Gainor Christ was a patron of McDaids pub in Dublin.

Donleavy's "Ginger Man," who goes by the name of Sebastian Dangerfield, is a young American ne'er-do-well student at Trinity College with a voracious appetite for wine, women, and song, which leads him to experience numerous misadventures in Dublin.

8. PATRICK JOSEPH KAVANAGH

A twentieth-century working-class parochial poet from County Monaghan, Kavanagh finally took up residence in Dublin around 1940 where he continued to write idealized lyrics of rural life while doing columns for the *Irish Press*.

He was a frequent patron of numerous Dublin pubs, and despite the care that he took to disparage the stereotypes of the Irish in his work, Kavanaugh nonetheless eventually evolved into one himself, the hard-drinking, pub-going Irish poet.

9. DARBY O'GILL

The fictional creation of Herminie T. Kavanagh (whose work was later immortalized in a Walt Disney film), Darby is the archetypal rural codger who has brushes with the supernatural only to have others discount his accounts as either tall tales or poteen-based hallucinations. The sprites themselves often bedevil him in secret, leaving his family and friends to wonder constantly if it's really demons or just the drink.

10. RAPHAEL HOLINSHED

Sixteenth-century chronicler who wrote (on the subject of Irish whiskey):

> "It keepeth the reason from stifling,
> the stomach from wambling,
> the heart from welling,
> the belliw from wirtchinh,
> the guts from numbling,
> the hands from shivering,
> the sinews from shrinking,
> the veines from crumpling,
> the bones from aking,
> and the marrow from soaking.
> And truly it is a sovereigne liquor
>   If it be orderlie taken."

Irish Delicacies

Irish cooking is always quite filling (who could name all of the uses for a potato?) and delicious as well as this list of Emerald Isle delicacies proves.

1. **IRISH SODA BREAD**

Whole meal flour, dash of oatmeal, dash of whole wheat, an egg, a spoon of baking soda, three-quarters pint of buttermilk, dash of regular milk, salt, sugar, raisins, and caraway seeds to taste. Mix as bread and bake at 450 degrees.

Fine for dessert, breakfast, or just as a snack.

2. **CORNED BEEF AND CABBAGE**

Combine the piece of corned beef with the cabbage in a single pot, bring to a boil, and simmer for twenty minutes per pound of beef. Enjoy the aroma during cooking.

3. IRISH STEW

Combine lamb chops (cut off the bone), potatoes, onions, carrots, dash of chopped parsley, a pint of water, and salt and pepper to taste.

Add all ingredients to a saucepan and bring to a boil, then reduce heat and simmer for two hours.

4. COLCANNON

Colcannon consists of cabbage, boiled potatoes, two leeks, a cup of milk, butter, and salt and pepper to taste.

Mash and mix the potatoes and seasonings, then top with milk before adding cabbage. Pile it into a dish, making a well in the center for a dollop of butter.

5. BAKED HAM

Steep ham overnight in cold water seasoned with cloves and pepper, then remove skin and coat with your choice of sweet breading (one good choice: honey and breadcrumbs with a touch of cloves).

Bake in moderate oven for forty minutes in three cups of cider, turning ham over midway through to avoid drying out one side.

6. CODDLE

Coddle contains ham sliced thick, pork sausage, sliced potatoes and onions, parsley, salt and pepper to taste, and two pints of boiling water.

Boil the meat for five minutes, strain and reserve. Add with vegetables to an ovenproof dish, moistening with reserved liquid from the boiling. Bake at 200 degrees for about an hour and you have yourself coddle.

7. **BOXTY POTATOES**

Grated raw potatoes, cooked mashed potatoes, flour, melted butter, and baking soda make up boxty pancakes.

Mix the grated potatoes with the mashed, adding the rest of the ingredients to make a batter. Then fry gently as pancakes and serve with butter.

8. **NETTLE SOUP**

Ingredients:

2½ parts nettles
Butter to taste
⅓ part oatmeal
3¾ parts stock
1¼ parts milk

Chop the nettle leaves thoroughly, removing the stalks. Mix butter and oatmeal, heat until golden brown. Add stock, bring to a boil, add milk, bring to a boil, add nettles, and simmer for another ten minutes.

9. **GUINNESS CAKE**

Ingredients:

1 cup butter
1 cup brown sugar
1¼ cups Guinness (not including excess for the cook to sample)
Raisins
Currants
Orange and lemon peel to taste
5 cups flour
3 pinches baking soda
Pinch each allspice and nutmeg
3 eggs

Mix butter, sugar, and Guinness in a pan and bring the mixture to a boil. Add the fruits and peels and simmer for an additional few minutes. Sift the flour and baking soda into a bowl; add the spices, fruit, Guinness mixture, and the three eggs, then beat until smooth.

Pour into a cake pan and bake for two hours at 325 degrees.

10. TRADITIONAL IRISH BREAKFAST

A "traditional" Irish breakfast includes the foods listed below, cooked to preference. Though tradition really demands that it all be fried in a pan, health/dietary concerns sometimes dictate otherwise.

2 slices Irish bacon
1 Irish sausage (also known as a banger)
1 slice black breakfast pudding
1 slice white breakfast pudding
1 tomato (cored)
Pepper to taste

It's a definite eye-opening delight, even if it does clog the arteries.

Rebel Songs

It is said that the troubled history of Ireland is forever enshrined in folk songs . . . and if you listen closely to the words of the riotous songs being sung as you pass an Irish bar on St. Patty's Day, you can't help but become melancholy over the lives lost in pursuit of independence. Some songs you can "hear" by looking at someone's arm, as "No, Never Again" (the author's favorite) has been turned into many a tattoo.

The best songs of Ireland are songs of rebellion, and new ones will be sung until the final day when true independence is won.

1. "A NATION ONCE AGAIN"

"A Nation Once Again" was written in the 1840s by Thomas Osbourne Davis, one of the founders of a group pressing for Ireland's independence. The song dreams of a time when Ireland will be a free land, exhorting its countrymen to rise up and fight. It's been recorded by many singers and groups, including the Irish Tenors, and in 2002 a BBC World Service poll listed it as the world's most popular tune.

2. "THE WILD COLONIAL BOY"

Apparently this song was very popular among Britain's colonies; three different versions are floating around—the Canadians and Australians have their own version of this Irish tune. It centers on one Jack Doolan, who seems to be an Irish version of Robin Hood, robbing the rich and giving to the poor. Outnumbered three-to-one and urged to surrender, Doolan instead drew two guns but was shot through the heart, killed, and captured only in death.

3. "BOLD FENIAN MEN"

Written around the time of the 1916 rebellion by Peader Kearney, this song commemorates earlier Irish uprisings. If you've ever seen the John Wayne movie, *Rio Grande*, then you've heard this song that celebrates the bravery of the Irish men who fought to the death because of their love for Ireland.

4. "THE WEARING OF THE GREEN"

"The Wearing of the Green" was written by Dion Boucicault, a playwright born in Dublin. Emboldened by America's successful revolution, many Irish thought the time was ripe for their independence as well. Green became the color to wear for those sympathetic to the cause, and, in response, the British outlawed the wearing of the green and executed those who transgressed. Boucicault's song was the Irish reply, asking if the green of grass, leaves, and the shamrock would soon be outlawed, too.

5. "JOHNNY, I HARDLY KNEW YE"

A traditional song dating from the early nineteenth century, "Johnny, I Hardly Knew Ye" was the basis for the American song "When Johnny Comes Marching Home." Some date it to the period after an 1802 treaty, when Irish soldiers were recruited for duty in East India. Unlike the celebration heard in the American version, the Irish song involves a fair colleen asking about Johnny's loss of arms, legs, and eyes.

6. "BLACK VELVET BAND"

There are a few different versions of this song, including "Blue Velvet Band" and "Black Ribbon Band," and the city in question can vary depending on where you are, but the message is the same: You can't trust women.

The singer meets a woman wearing a black velvet band in her hair, and the two party the night away. At some point she slips him a watch she'd stolen, and the two are arrested for her theft. He's sentenced to seven years in prison, closing the song with a warning for the men out there to beware of following the black velvet band.

7. "THE PATRIOT GAME"

Written by Dominic Behan, "The Patriot Game" tells the story of one Fergal O'Hanlon, killed in battle at the tender age of sixteen. The "game," of course, is fighting for Ireland's independence. The second half of the song seems to criticize the deserters, those who joined the game but turned "traitor" and "sold out" the cause, according to the song.

8. "THE WIND THAT SHAKES THE BARLEY"

Written by Robert Dwyer Joyce in the nineteenth century, "The Wind that Shakes the Barley" commemorates the uprising of 1798. In it, a young man debates between his two true loves, one a woman and the other Ireland. While telling his girlfriend of his need to go and fight, she's killed in his arms, solidifying his desire to join the battle. The singer even realizes what his fate will likely be, placing her in a grave where he says he "soon will follow."

9. "SCAFFOLD PASSAGE"

"Scaffold Passage" is based on Robert Emmet's last words. In 1803 Emmett attempted to seize Dublin Castle but was caught and executed. His last words in a speech before his execution were an instruction that no man should write his epitaph until Ireland was free.

10. "COME OUT, YE BLACK AND TANS"

Another song by Dominic Behan (who also wrote "The Patriot Game"), "Come Out Ye Black and Tans" tells of a man who would call out the British, the "black and tans," to come and face him like a man and tell of all the people they've oppressed, while promising one day that the Irish will rise above.

Heroes of Legend and History

Irish men are always ready for a fight or a frolic, but mostly they are ready to defend the honor and integrity of their own. In legend and history the bold Irish hero is a recurring figure, in the early years of the isle as well as in current history.

1. CÚ CHULAINN

Cú Chulainn is a legendary Celtic hero of the first century whose exploits are featured in the Ulster cycle (the most famous of which is *The Cattle Raid of Cooley*). Also known as Culann's hound, he is a simple man of great strength and fierce cunning who survived numerous battles in this world and the otherworld.

2. FINN MACCOOL

MacCool was a legendary Fenian hero based on an actual general who organized an Irish regular army in the third century. According to the cycle of tales surrounding MacCool's exploits, his most atypical behavior was gaining knowledge by chewing on his thumb.

3. BRIAN BORU

King of Munster and high king of Ireland from 1001 to 1014, Boru was the first chieftain to attain dominion over almost the entire isle. Although his military and political accomplishments were numerous, he was also a builder of churches and forts and a patron of the arts.

4. "STRONGBOW"

Richard de Clare, the Earl of Pembroke and Striguil in the twelfth century, known as "Strongbow," was of Anglo-Norman descent and, at the request of the exiled king of Leinster, led a victorious attack on Dublin in the fall of 1170.

5. OWEN ROE O'NEILL

After the flight of the earls O'Neill, this younger brother of Hugh O'Neill (second Earl of Tyrone) returned out of exile to Ireland to lead an army for the Confederation of Kilkenny in the rebellion of 1640.

6. PATRICK SARSFIELD

The first Earl of Lucan, Sarsfield led the siege of Limerick in 1691 with only five hundred troops, and by means of a daring raid on William III's supply train, destroyed all of the king's munitions.

7. WOLFE TONE

Eighteenth-century father of Irish Republicanism, Wolfe Tone founded the United Irishmen in Belfast in 1791 and was a prime instigator of the rebellion of 1798. He committed suicide rather than allowing himself to be executed by hanging, after which he was to have been drawn and quartered.

8. ROBERT EMMET

Wolfe Tone's protégé, Emmet staged an abortive revolt in 1803 by trying to seize Dublin Castle. He was captured and sentenced to the fate from which Tone had escaped.

9. MICHAEL COLLINS

A founder and director of intelligence of the Irish Republican Army (IRA) in 1919, this County Cork–born son of a farmer led a ruthless guerrilla war against the British following the failure of the 1916 Easter Rising, with targeted assassinations and infiltration of British intelligence.

Due to political fallout with others in the IRA, he merged as the commander in chief of the National army and head of the Irish Free State in 1922 for ten days before he was assassinated on the orders of one of his former comrades in arms.

He was immortalized on screen in the eponymous film by Neal Jordan with Liam Neeson giving his all to fill the boots of the "big fellow."

10. GERRY ADAMS

Belfast-born president of Sinn Fein who became involved with Northern Ireland politics at a very early age, Adams was allegedly given his first IRA command (the Second Battalion, Belfast Brigade) at the age of twenty-three in 1971, the height of the Troubles.

He was elected to Parliament but declined his seat as he refused to take an oath of allegiance to the British queen.

He is, some say, the new Moses who will lead his people to true independence.

Legendary Lasses

Despite the unfortunate antifeminism of the Roman Catholic faith, many lasses have achieved legendary status in their service to the Emerald Isle and the world. Irish colleens are far from shy, descended from powerfully strong goddesses and ready to make their opinions known and their force and strength felt, even when they exercise a certain lack of judgment not unlike their male counterparts.

1. DANU (OR DANANN)

Danu, the mother goddess of Celtic mythology, represents the land and all of the wonders of nature in this pagan faith and shares an ancestry with her portfolio counterpart in Indo-European culture. (Indeed, the Danube River is probably named after Danu's soul sister.)

As Celtic/Irish culture evolved, her powers increased to make her the de facto goddess of war (it's not nice to fool Mother Nature), and many believe she provided the basis for both the Arthurian Morgan le Fey and certain of the legendary qualities of St. Brigid, as well as the role of phantom queen in the hero tales of the Tuatha de Danaan. A very busy legendary lass if, indeed, she existed.

2. LADY GREGORY

Born Isabella Augusta Persse, this legendary lady of the Irish cultural renaissance was both a patron and an artist in her own right whose works inspired many, only possibly surpassed by the number of people she inspired in person.

Lady Gregory's plays include *Grania* (a drama of an ancient Irish female sea captain), *Rising of the Moon*, and *Gaol Gate*, and she wrote numerous articles and an autobiography.

As a patron she was integral to the founding of the Abbey Theatre in Dublin and was an intimate soul mate of William Butler Yeats, whose work she encouraged by sharing with him her love of Irish culture. They remained lifelong friends, though Yeats desired much more exclusivity in their relationship.

3. MAUD GONNE

This founder of the Daughters of Ireland and original founding member of Sinn Fein is the true mother of Independent and Free Ireland. Gonne brought the cause onto the world stage by preaching about Irish nationalism even though she wasn't even born in Ireland.

A social bohemian who nonetheless maintained a station in the upper class, Gonne had many lovers and was a muse/lover of several members of the Irish renaissance, including William Butler Yeats, a lifelong friend. Again it was obvious that Yeats desired more in the manner of exclusivity in their relationship. Once Yeats broke off their relationship, Gonne married John McBride, but only long enough to bear his son.

She was an active participant in the early days of resistance following the Rising and maintained an active profile in Irish politics into her seventies.

4. MOTHER JONES

The seminal Irish battleaxe of the American labor movement, Irish-born Mary Jones had moved to America and was already in her fifties when she became a firebrand of the American labor movement, earning several bouts of incarceration for civil disobedience and labor demonstrations well unto her ninetieth year.

5. CONSTANCE MARKIEVICZ

Sometimes known as the Red Countess, this Sligo lass was educated in London and Paris of finer schools, which allowed her to become acquainted with and wed the Polish count, Casimir Markievicz. Her newfound Polish nobility did not distract her from the cause, however; she joined Sinn Fein in 1908 and helped found the republican youth organization, Na Fianna, the following year.

A "very" close friend of Maud Gonne, she eventually became head of the Irish Women Worker's Union and even took part in the Easter Rising (for which she was arrested and would have been condemned to death if she hadn't been of Polish nobility).

Markievicz was also elected as the first British female member of Parliament (MP) but refused to serve, instead opting to serve as Labor Minister in the outlawed Republican parliament.

6. ALICE KYTELER

Also known as Dame Alice, Kyteler had married and outlived four husbands and in doing so had amassed a sizeable fortune, which allowed her a degree of independence that led her to run afoul of the archbishop of Ossory. It being the fourteenth century, the archbishop twice charged her with witchcraft for her arrogant (by today's standards "feminist") ways and attempted to have her burned at the stake.

With the advantage of her fortune, Alice was able to escape to England to avoid the executioner, leaving her son to be arrested and another woman to be executed in her place, the first such witch execution recorded in Irish history. The odd woman, Dame Alice, on the other hand, was never heard from again.

7. CHRISTIEN DAVIES

She was a Dublin-born, seventeenth-century transvestite who went to war in search of her conscripted husband and under the name of Christopher Walsh, seeing action at the Battle of Blenheim.

In total she married three times, all military men, outliving each and every one of them. She eventually died in her early seventies, spending her final years in Chelsea Pensioners Hospital for Retired Soldiers.

8. MARY AIKENHEAD

What would a list of legendary lasses be without a goodly nun? Sister Mary Aikenhead founded the Irish Sisters of Charity (the first order of its kind on the Emerald Isle), even though she was raised as a Protestant in County Cork until the fortuitous death of her father allowed to convert at the age of sixteen.

She entered the convent after her mother's demise, trained in England, then returned to Ireland where she established her order at North William Street in Dublin and served as its mother superior.

9. BERNADETTE DEVLIN-MCALISKEY

Born Bernadette Devlin in 1947, this young, five-foot-tall firebrand and Northern Ireland activist was elected to Parliament at the age of twenty-one (the youngest MP since William Pitt), and shortly thereafter was arrested for leading a group of Catholic rioters in Londonderry.

Targeted for assassination several times, she faded from sight soon thereafter, though she continued to chair the Independent Socialist Party of Ireland.

10. SINEAD O'CONNOR

It's not because she has the voice of an angel and the distinctive "bald chick" look that helped to drive her image and acclaim with hits like Prince's "Nothing Compares 2 U" or "The Emperor's New Clothes," nor is it that she followed up her successful pop/rock first album with a collection of Cole Porter (and others) show tunes, nor that she embraced lesbianism, then got married to a man and had a child, and then reembraced old Irish religions. The real reason O'Connor made this list is that at the height of her pop stardom she appeared on the hit show, *Saturday Night Live*, and ripped up a photo of Pope John Paul II on live TV, earning the enmity of Catholics and others around the world.

What could she possibly have been thinking? It doesn't matter; with that moment she achieved pop infamy.

Silver-Tongued Orators

It is said that the Irish are blessed with the gift of gab and a touch of the blarney—easy to talk to and with whether in a pub, on the street, or on your way to a police station (usually as you try to talk your brother-in-blarney out of taking you in). This is not to say, however, that the gift only extends to informal conversation.

The Irish are equally silver-tongued in public speaking, particularly in matters concerning the fate of Ireland or, in some cases, one's own safety, freedom, or survival.

1. ARTHUR GRIFFITH (1872–1922)

Born in Dublin and a printer by trade, Griffith, who founded Sinn Fein, was part of the fivesome that negotiated the treaty with Britain in 1921, only to have it voted down by de Valera and his followers upon their return to Ireland.

Griffith realized that the treaty had many negatives attached to it, but nonetheless saw it as a positive step

Arthur Griffith, founder of Sinn Fein.

toward securing Irish independence and stopping the bloodshed and oppression. His impassioned defense of the treaty as the best alternative for Ireland at the time led to its ratification by a narrow majority. Unfortunately, it also led to the Irish Civil War.

2. GEORGE BERNARD SHAW (1856-1950)

This Dublin-born master playwright and critic was also a founding force in the socialist-leaning Fabian Society founded by Sidney and Beatrice Webb, which afforded him numerous opportunities to extol the virtues of Marxism to the middle classes. As Shaw's reputation as an intellectual, artist, and curmudgeon grew, he was in great demand as a speaker, both after dinner and on the radio.

Whether his thrust was positive and praising (as in his speech on the genius, Albert Einstein, in 1930) or negative and nasty (as were his usual responses to his critics), Shaw always managed to hold his audience in the palm of his hand, even when its members didn't agree with him.

3. EAMON DE VALERA (1882-1975)

Architect of the Rising of 1916 and eventually president of Ireland, this statesman's statesman was as eloquent a speaker as he was elegant a writer. Particularly noteworthy moments of his oratory excellence took place during the late thirties and early forties when he boldly advocated Irish neutrality in World War II. He was unafraid to express his opinion to the masses, to the airwaves, and even to the great bulldog orator himself, Winston Churchill.

4. EDMUND BURKE (1729-1797)

Born and educated in Dublin, Burke became a practicing politician in London and once delivered a four-day-long opening speech in Westminster Hall at the onset of an impeachment hearing. His essays, "On American Taxation," "Conciliation with America," and "Reflections on the Revolution in France," are all considered classics, though this oratorical firebrand had more of an effect on the revolutions in America and France than he did on the welfare of the land of his birth.

5. CHARLES STEWART PARNELL (1846-1891)

As a member of Parliament in 1875, Parnell achieved great notoriety with his creative obstructionism, which included all-night filibusters to draw attention to the Irish problem.

Whether Parnell spoke at length on the floor of the House of Commons, on the road in the United States in search of support for the Irish people, or at a common meeting in Ireland, the desire for a free Irish republic never had a better spokesman or a more ingenious advocate.

6. JOHN A. COSTELLO (1891-1976)

Costello was a conspirator in the 1916 Rising, attorney general for the Irish Free State, and de Valera's successor as Irish prime minister.

In his Introductory Speech on the Republic of Ireland Act on November 24, 1948, Costello urged the country to complete its evolution to republic status, recognizing they already had done so with Britain in all but name. Though no de Valera, Costello nonetheless achieved his goals.

7. ROGER CASEMENT (1864—1916)

The son of a British army officer, Casement didn't ally himself with the nationalist movement until he retired from the colonial services in 1913, after having been knighted by the Crown in 1911. His oratory excellence is based primarily on his June 30, 1916, statement in court defending himself against the charges of treason against the Crown. Casement's statement offered not just his own personal explanation, but rather an explanation of and vindication for the rebellion of all Irishmen, laying out the history of the Crown's crimes and tyrannies and the rationale for rebellion against the Crown.

The moving speech offered a solid argument, but Casement was hanged for treason shortly after.

8. DANIEL O'CONNELL (1775-1847)

Born in Kerry, O'Connell was the first Irish Catholic member of British Parliament and a firebrand who led his people in peaceful agitation. O'Connell's oratorical gifts were evidenced by his eloquence on the floor of Parliament in his "Speech Against Coercive Legislation" and his passionate speech at the seat of the ancient high kings on August 15, 1843, when he condemned the Act of Union and called for its repeal.

9. JOHN DILLON (1851-1927)

Though trained as a doctor, Dillon embraced politics as an MP for County Tipperary and became a leader of the anti-Parnell camp after the 1871 split in the Irish Nationalist Party. Once the party had been reunited, Dillon temporarily became its head, only to lose to de Valera in the subsequent election. His firebrand speech on the floor of the House of Commons on May 11 after the April 1916 Rising was a warning to stop the military executions that were taking place or the formerly fractured faction of Sinn Fein rebels would become the voice of the majority of downtrodden Dubliners.

10. JONATHAN SWIFT (1667-1745)

The legendary Dean Swift was as powerful from the pulpit of St. Patrick's Cathedral as his satiric pen was mighty. As matters became heated during the dispute of 1720 concerning Parliament's legal jurisdiction over Ireland, Swift used his sermons to hammer home his points, sometimes mixing Biblical phrases with his arguments, as he did with his "Causes of the Wretched Condition of Ireland," which he introduced with a recitation of Psalm 144, verses 13 and 14.

Irish Men
of the Cloth

In a culture so driven by conflicts of religion and faith, it is only proper that members of the clergy occasionally set themselves apart from the crowd, and, as with all walks of life, some are heroes, some are villains, and some are just comic relief . . . and, of course, others are the stuff of which legends are made.

1. FATHER EDWARD JOSEPH FLANAGAN

Born in Ballaghaderreen, County Roscommon, Flanagan moved to the United States in 1904 and was ordained a priest in 1914. He started a homeless shelter in Nebraska, which later led to his greatest claim to fame: creating Boys Town, with its famous epithets, "He ain't heavy, he's my brother" and "There is no such thing as a bad boy."

The success of this remarkable institution led to international fame and two films in which Spencer Tracy portrayed Flanagan.

He was on a post–World War II tour of Japan and Germany promoting Boys Town projects for the postwar era when he died at the age of sixty-two.

2. FATHER O'MALLEY

One of Bing Crosby's most memorable portrayals was as the easygoing, crooning priest, Father O'Malley, in the movies, *Going My Way*, and its sequel, *The Bells of Saint Mary's*. Despite his Anglo-Irish background, O'Malley is the perfect precursor to Vatican II (close to twenty years in the future) with his pragmatic ways and young, dare I say "hip," way of dealing with traditional matters of the cloth.

It is noteworthy that O'Malley's superior in *Going My Way* was played by the even more Irish Barry Fitzgerald, who holds a special place in record books as the only person to have been nominated for both Best Actor and Best Supporting Actor for the same part in the same movie (he won the Supporting Actor award, at which point they changed the rules so such a thing could never happen again).

3. FATHER ALEC REID

This unassuming Redemptorist father of Belfast was one of the great behind-the-scenes peacemakers of the Good Friday Accords, having come to prominence through numerous photos of him caring for the wounded, dead, and dying in the streets of Belfast during the carnage of the frequent exchanges between IRA gunmen and British soldiers. His subtle actions helped to bring about the cease-fire in 1994, and he frequently acted as a go-between twixt Gerry Adams and Social Democratic and Labour Party (SDLP) leader John Hume.

Reid is undaunted by the Unionist devils standing in the way of peace and has faith that one Ireland, Catholic and Protestant, will prevail over the hate.

4. FATHER FRANCIS P. DUFFY

Immortalized on screen by Pat O'Brien in *The Fighting 69th*, Father Francis P. Duffy, chaplain of 69th Rainbow Division out of Brooklyn (mostly Irish Americans) who valiantly fought in World War I, portrayed his frontline experiences in his memoir, *Father Duffy's Story*. Among his parishioners both at home and abroad was the poet Joyce Kilmer, author of the poem, "Trees."

5. CARDINAL CAHAL DALY

Born in Loughguile, Ireland, in 1917, this Catholic bishop (later cardinal) wrote several books preaching Christian unity, hoping to act as a voice of reason among the faith-driven warring factions of Northern Ireland.

He always attempted to refrain from "political speak," but he broke from this in July 1996 and essentially emerged as the "anti-Paisley" (see Ian Paisley entry below) by condemning the divisive and violent marches of the Protestant Orange Order, which he saw as the British authorities' betrayal of the peace process to forestall negotiations.

6. FATHER JERRY CONNOLLY

As Father Jerry Connolly, Pat O'Brien once again played a priest from the wrong side of the tracks and boyhood friend of a ruthless gangster in the movie, *Angels with Dirty Faces*. O'Brien emerged as the road-not-taken alternative to the archetypal James Cagney kid-of-the-streets-turned–gangster, William "Rocky" Sullivan, or as the old cliché says, "There but for the grace of God go I." Indeed, Connolly returns to the old neighborhood to save a new generation of delinquents from a career of criminality and even convinces his old friend to "go quietly" so he won't be remembered as a hero and serve as an inspiration for a new generation of gangsters.

7. REVEREND IAN PAISLEY

Hate-mongering leader of the Democratic Unionist Party, this Baptist minister, who preached his first sermon at the age of sixteen, established the Free Presbyterian Church of Ulster in Belfast where he consistently invoked the Lord's name as an endorsement of his anti-Catholic sentiments.

Through both elected politics and Anglo-Protestant terrorist activities (including a disruption at an address by Pope John Paul II) Paisley's anti-Catholic/anti-Irish independence message has been a consistent roadblock to Irish peace talks from the early Troubles of the '60s through the Good Friday Accords.

According to Paisley, "No surrender" (in response to calls for Irish independence) and "I would rather be British than just," which probably casts some doubts on his compassion and clerical status.

8. FATHER CHARLES COUGHLIN

Hate-mongering cleric of the 1920s and 1930s on the other side of the Atlantic, this Irish Canadian used his weekly radio broadcasts throughout the United States (with one-third of the U.S. population tuned in each week) to preach economic reform (beyond that advocated by the Roosevelt administration) and severe anti-Semitism.

Probably the only group he hated more than the Jews was the Protestants in Ireland. In 1940 his superiors finally recognized the vitriol he was spewing and forced him off the air and back into service as a parish priest.

9.   THE ASSORTED CLERICS OF *BALLYKISSANGEL* AND *FATHER TED*

Whether portraying an earnest young cleric who has just come to town to serve God and his flock on earth, a brother who's the brother of a liberated lass, or just an over-the-top caricature of Irish popery, these programs together run the gamut of stereotypes of "the Irish men of the cloth."

10.   BISHOP PATRICK (ALSO CALLED ST. PATRICK)

And, of course, there's Bishop Patrick, the poster boy for all things religious and Irish. 'Nuff said.

Irish Novelists

As the written word is prized among the Irish people, the novels produced by the artisans of the Emerald Isle are as wide ranging as Irish culture itself, hallowed in tradition yet unafraid of breaking conventions in genre and content.

1. JAMES JOYCE

Born in Dublin in 1882 and educated at University College, James Joyce is regarded as Ireland's most influential novelist if not the most influential novelist of the entire twentieth century. Through his novelized stream of consciousness technique (which had already been so successful in poetry), Joyce revolutionized the fiction genre, allowing its narration to range as wide as the limits of the human mind through its content and technique (which caused more than a stir of trouble among the more genre's conservative practitioners).

The lack of acceptance of his work led him into exile in France before moving to Switzerland, where he died in 1941 from complications of abdominal surgery.

His major works include *The Portrait of the Artist as a Young Man* (considered to be largely autobiographical), *Ulysses* (an eventful day in Dublin patterned after Homer's epic *The Odyssey*), and *Finnegan's Wake*.

2. JONATHAN SWIFT

Born in Dublin in 1667, Dean Swift is truly Ireland's Grand Master of Letters. A noted satirist and pamphleteer (among other notable accomplishments), Swift is best known for *Gulliver's Travels*, his famous picaresque satire of the journeys of a sea captain named Gulliver whose travels bring him to lands of people big and small, scientifically smart and commonsense stupid, and, of course, the highly intelligent, civilized talking horses.

3. JOHN BANVILLE

Born in Wexford, Banville wrote for the *Irish Press* and served as literary editor of the *Irish Times* before striking it big as a literary novelist in his own right by mixing science, history, and politics into morality play–driven works of fiction involving intellectually complex characters.

His major works include *Doctor Copernicus* (from his men of science sequence), *Mefisto*, *The Book of Evidence* (a thinking man's book of crime reminiscent of Dostoyevsky's themes), *Ghosts*, and *Athena, A Novel*.

4. MORGAN LLEWELYN

Though born in New York City of Irish and Welsh-Irish parents, Llewelyn is an Irish citizen and has even served as the chairman of the Irish Writers Union. In addition to being an internationally best-selling author of Irish historical fiction, she is perhaps the only woman ever to have walked the length and breadth of the Emerald Isle, from Malin Head to Mizen Head.

Her major works include *The Wind from Hastings*, *Lion of God* (on King Brian Boru), *The Horse Goddess*, *Bard*, and *1916* (the first book in her sequence covering twentieth-century Irish history).

5. RODDY DOYLE

Born in Dublin and educated at University College, Doyle has enjoyed considerable success with his novels that depict life in Ireland, ranging from sitcom style slices of life to autobiographical novels to novelized history, including several film adaptations and a 1993 Booker Prize.

His major works include *The Commitments* (which was made into a memorable Alan Parker film), *Paddy Clarke Ha Ha Ha* (which won the Booker prize), *The Woman Who Walked Into Doors*, and *A Star Called Henry* (the first book in a sequence of historical novels, "the Last Round-up").

6. BERNARD MACLAVERTY

Born in Belfast, MacLaverty worked as a medical technician before turning to a life of letters and subsequently moved to Scotland. In 1983 *Cal* (made into a movie with Helen Mirren) brought his work to the world's attention. Like several of his stories, this lyrical novel explores the situation in Northern Ireland. Other major works include *Lamb* and *Grace Notes*.

7. CHARLES ROBERT MATURIN

Born of Huguenot descent in Dublin, Maturin was educated at Trinity College and ordained as a minister in 1803. His religious vocation, however, in no way impeded his becoming one of the leading lights of the gothic novel movement that started with Horace Walpole's *The Castle of Otranto.*

His major works include *Fatal Revenge: or the Family of Montario*, *The Milesian Chief*, *Bertram*, and *Melmoth the Wanderer* (the last is considered by many learned scholars to be the greatest gothic novel of all time).

8. BRAM STOKER

Born in Dublin and educated at Trinity College, Stoker started a civil service career before accepting a position as personal assistant/manager to the actor, Sir Henry Irving. Today, however, he is primarily remembered as the creator of the most famous vampire of all time.

His major works include *The Lair of the White Worm* (the basis for a very kinky Amanda Donahoe and Hugh Grant film directed by Ken Russell), *The Jewel of the Seven Stars* (which was filmed as *The Blood from the Mummy's Tomb* and again as *The Awakening* with Charlton Heston), and, of course, *Dracula.*

9. MAURICE WALSH

Born in County Kerry, Walsh was schooled in Ireland, later moved to Scotland, then returned to Ireland in 1922. His works drew from both settings and histories, and one of his shorter novels provided the basis for the classic John Wayne-John Ford film, *The Quiet Man.*

Other major works include *The Key Above the Door* and *Sons of the Swordmaker.*

10. **MAEVE BINCHY**

Born in Dublin and educated at University College, Binchy started her career as a teacher and travel writer before joining the *Irish Times* in 1969. Her major works, which often take place in Dublin, include *Light a Penny Candle*, *Firefly Summer*, *Circle of Friends* (filmed with Minnie Driver and Chris O'Donnell), *Evening Class*, and *Tara Road.*

narratives
of Ireland

In a land of storytellers, which is what Ireland can truly claim to be, it would be an injustice to limit the scope of a writer's tale to a single novel. Indeed, most of the prominent authors of the Emerald Isle prefer to write large with narratives continuing over several volumes.

Though each book may have a self-contained plot, nonetheless, the narrative—like the road before the Irish people—continues to go ever on, allowing the fictional master a canvas wide as the eye can read.

1. *PORTRAIT OF THE ARTIST AS A YOUNG MAN, ULYSSES, AND FINNEGAN'S WAKE* **BY JAMES JOYCE**

In addition to Joyce's stream-of-consciousness masterworks setting the bar higher for all later works of the twentieth century, these three novels form an unmistakably Irish trilogy dealing with such taboo subjects as religion, sex, and man's place in society (as well as such other themes as growing up, friendship, and betrayal).

Even when the books are reduced to their simplest themes, such as the story of Stephen Daedalus's education, disillusionment, and development as an artist in Catholic, repressive Ireland or Leopold Bloom's one-day walk around Dublin, these narratives capture an Ireland in transition at the dawn of a new century.

2. *THE YEAR OF THE FRENCH, THE TENANTS OF TIME,* AND *THE END OF THE HUNT* BY THOMAS FLANAGAN

Flanagan's historical romantic epic traces the years of rebellion from the so-called Year of the French 1798, through the days of Parnell and the rising of 1867, right up to the era of Michael Collins and the birth of the Irish Republican Army.

Flanagan mixes real historical figures with characters of his own invention to convey the human side of epic events.

3. *IRISH FAIRY AND FOLK TALES* EDITED BY WILLIAM BUTLER YEATS

Yeats compiled this collection for publication in 1892 and tried to include examples from all realms of Irish mythos. Yeats had started studying these works in recognition of their key contribution to the oeuvre that would form the basis of the Irish literary revival. From stories of faeries, ghosts, and wee folk, to more religious-oriented message tales of priests and demons, Yeats's volume was a landmark work of the Irish fantastic and an Emerald Isle alternative to *Bulfinch's Mythology*.

4. *1916, 1921, 1949, 1972,* AND *1999* BY MORGAN LLEWELYN

Llewelyn has constructed a tightly plotted cycle of novels that trace major twentieth-century events in

Ireland through the microcosm of five tipping-point years.

As she did with mythic Irish history in such books as *Lion of Ireland*, *Grania*, and *Bard*, Llewelyn fully documents her source material to impart a sense of historic reality to the events at hand. This is history as seen by witnesses whose legacies influence future generations, and it is fine, historic storytelling as well.

5. THE CYCLES OF LORE

Four hero cycles emerging from early Irish folklore resulted in connected sets of hero tales of the great warriors of the past.

The *Mythological Cycle* deals with pre-Celtic gods and heroes, the Irish answer to Valhalla and Olympus; the *Ulster Cycle* contains the tales of the Red Branch Knights of Navan Fort and their champion, Cú Chulainn; the *Fenian Cycle* highlights Finn MacCool, alleged builder of the Giant's Causeway; and the *Cycle of Kings* merges with recorded history and mirrors the Avalon tales of the Irish kings' British brethren.

All four are tales in the oral tradition filled with exciting battles and larger-than-life heroes who border on humanity and the fairy realm. It is from these strong early tales that the mythos of Irish nationalism evolved.

6. *THE BARRYTOWN TRILOGY* BY RODDY DOYLE

Moving from the mythology-oriented tales of hero warriors of the Cycles, Roddy Doyle embraces the light-hearted heroes of everyday life in his three Barrytown novels featuring the very working–class, ordinary Rabbitte family: *The Commitments*, the story of an Irish blues band trying to make it from working-class beginnings (later filmed by Alan Parker of *Midnight*

Express and *Fame* fame); *The Snapper*, the tale of an unwed mother-to-be and her family; and *The Van*, a get-rich-quick scheme revolving around a "chips" van.

Each novel provides a slice of life and hard times with a smile that reinforces the resiliency of the Irish working class.

7.   *THE LAST ROUNDUP* BY RODDY DOYLE

Only the first volume in this intended historical trilogy has been published to date. *A Star Called Henry* follows the loss of innocence of an Irish lad who becomes a gunman during the Easter Rising and subsequent years. If the first book is any indication of the quality of the rest, both are worth anticipating as Doyle tells the story of Irish independence.

8.   *LAMB, CAL,* AND *GRACE NOTES* BY BERNARD MACLAVERTY

These three novels by Belfast born and bred MacLaverty form a triptych involving issues of faith and identity in modern Ireland, from a boy's crisis of faith in Catholic school, to a young IRA gunman's loss of innocence and tragic love affair, to a talented young woman's quest to be an artist despite the social restrictions and antifeminist mindset that surrounds her.

9.   PETER MCGARR SERIES BY BARTHOLOMEW GILL

With titles like *The Death of a Joyce Scholar*, *Irish Seawolf*, *Irish Tinker*, and the last volume, *Death in Dublin*, Gill has enraptured multitudes of mystery fans with his Irish police procedurals featuring Chief Superintendent Peter McGarr of the Garda Siochana.

The noble inspector ventures all over Dublin and the surrounding countryside to solve his cases, with Gill bringing to life the little details of everyday Ireland.

10. THE IRISH RM STORIES OF SOMERVILLE AND ROSS

Written by Violet Martin and Edith Somerville at the turn of the century, these tales by two daughters of Galway and Cork relate the adventures of Major Sinclair Yates, the Rural Magistrate. They are filled with whimsy and local lore that have set the standard for Anglo rural comedies for years to come, along with the memorable eccentrics and lighthearted humor noticeably lacking the brewing unrest to come in twentieth-century Ireland.

Memoirs of the Old Sod

Though life on the Emerald Isle has been evoked beautifully in poems, plays, and fiction, perhaps the memoir most easily brings it to life on the printed page. Sometimes the tale teller evokes nostalgia, sometimes catharsis, but always a little bit of memory brought to life.

From the wide array of volumes deserving mention, here are ten such lives on the printed page.

1. *ANGELA'S ASHES* BY FRANK MCCOURT

This Pulitzer Prize–winning memoir of a family of Irish immigrants who return to the old sod and the slums of Limerick relates how young Frank must come to terms with the hard life among the lowly with a father given to the drink and abandonment, brothers and sisters always on the verge of starvation and death, and his own bout with disease and dysfunction.

The story is continued in the second volume, *'Tis*, which picks up with McCourt's return to the land of his birth, America.

2. *FALL MEMORIES: A BELFAST LIFE* **AND** *CAGE ELEVEN* **BY GERRY ADAMS**

Fall Memories covers the patriot and patriarch of Sinn Fein's early years as the eldest of ten brothers and sisters in 1950s and '60s Belfast, and *Cage Eleven* tells of his inhumane internment on a prison ship during the 1970s as a political prisoner of the British government.

Together these two volumes provide an insightful look into the mind and life of one of New Ireland's founding fathers.

3. *ARE YOU SOMEBODY? THE ACCIDENTAL MEMOIR OF A DUBLIN WOMAN* **BY NUALA O'FAOLAIN**

One of nine children born in a penniless North Dublin family headed by an overwhelmed mother and a charming but absent father, O'Faolain not only survived but pushed at the boundaries of the confining Catholic Ireland in which she grew up. This work offers both a wonderfully nostalgic perspective of Ireland and a disturbing view of absent feminism on the Emerald Isle. O'Faolain continues her story in *Almost There.*

4. *AUTOBIOGRAPHIES* **BY WILLIAM BUTLER YEATS**

Autobiographies consists of six autobiographical works that William Butler Yeats published together in the mid-1930s to form a single, extraordinary memoir of the first fifty-eight years of his life, from his earliest memories of childhood through his Abbey Theatre years, the Nationalism movement, right up to his Nobel Prize for Literature.

5. *GUERRILLA DAYS IN IRELAND* **BY TOM BARRY**

An extraordinary memoir of the Anglo-Irish War, this work traces the development, augmentation, and implementation of the Irish Republican Army's "Flying Column" in Cork against the dreaded Black and Tans by the column's commander, a true hero of the cause.

6. *MY LEFT FOOT* BY CHRISTY BROWN

Though by no means typical, this memoir by the son of a Dublin bricklayer is both inspiring and evocative, not just because the author is stricken with cerebral palsy and writes with his left foot, but because of its optimism and wit at a time when medical knowledge of his condition was far from enlightened. It also provided the basis for a wonderful film of the same name.

7. *IT'S A LONG WAY FROM PENNY APPLES* BY BILL CULLEN

It's a Long Way from Penny Apples is a marvelous Horatio Alger–like account of Cullen's journey from the Summerhill, Dublin, slums to the ranks of the ten most successful businessmen in all of Ireland.

8. *ROSSA'S RECOLLECTIONS, 1838-1898: MEMOIRS OF AN IRISH REVOLUTIONARY* BY JEREMIAH O'DONOVAN ROSSA

This detailed personal account of nineteenth-century Irish patriot and revolutionary O'Donovan Rossa traces his early boyhood growing up on his grandfather's farm in Reanascreena; his thirteen-year imprisonment for involvement in the Fenian movement; and, finally, his exile to America, where he continued his activities in support of Irish independence. Through the work a portrait emerges of Ireland in the mid- to late 1800s, revealing what life was truly like for the Irish people.

9. *MOTHER IRELAND* BY EDNA O'BRIEN

Edna O'Brien describes growing up in rural County Clare, from her days in a convent school, to her first kiss, to her eventual move to England and beyond. Weaving her own personal history with that of Ireland, she melds local customs and lore with tales of the fascinating people and events that shaped her life.

10. ***THE MOUNTAIN OF THE WOMEN: MEMOIRS OF AN IRISH TROUBADOR* BY LIAM CLANCY**

Born in 1935, the last of eleven children, young Liam Clancy was an innocent lad of the Old Country. His childhood memories, which include bounding over hills, streams, and the occasional mountain; getting lost and, eventually, found; and making mischief in the way of a typical Irish boy, soon give way to the raucously funny and star-studded account of his move from provincial Ireland to the bars and clubs of New York City, to fame as a member of the Clancy Brothers and Tommy Makem.

Poets, Playwrights, and Pamphleteers

The annals of Irish culture are told in poems and lyrical cycles whence the Irish creative spirit was born and continued to thrive for centuries. Musical, yet sharp, the poets and playwrights expressed the true voice of the oppressed and the underlying spirit of freedom of the Irish people.

It is ironic that, once freedom was won or oppression overcome, the artists turned to nostalgia for an Ireland that never existed in the real worlds, only in their hearts.

1. WILLIAM BUTLER YEATS

Born a Protestant in 1865 Dublin, Yeats is considered by many to be the patriarch of the so-called Irish literary revival and one of the key founders of what would become the Abbey Theatre.

Yeats was a rarity at the time, a nationalist with no interest in active politics (despite his great affection for firebrand Maud Gonne, to whom he dedicated much of his poetry, as well as his service as a senator of the

Irish Free State). The nationalism he pursued was one of the Irish spirit/heart, which he evoked so lyrically in his work, for which he was awarded the Nobel Prize in 1923. Indeed, Yeats pioneered another trend among the Irish literati of his time—he left the Emerald Isle for France, where he eventually died.

Among his major works are *The Wanderings of Ossin and Other Poems*, *Deirdre*, *The Second Coming*, *The Tower*, and *Dramatis Personae*.

2. OSCAR WILDE

Born in 1854 Dublin to a successful eye surgeon and a literary doyenne, Wilde studied at Dublin and Oxford and basically became a poster boy for the "art for art's sake" movement. After dabbling with poetry and fairy tales, the young aesthete found his voice with his one novel, *The Picture of Dorian Gray*, and his exceptional plays of manners, morality, and decadence.

A scandalous affair and lawsuit led to Wilde's imprisonment, financial ruin, and eventual social ostracism. He died in Paris, an exile from the homeland for which he still had many nationalistic feelings.

Among his major works are *The Importance of Being Earnest*, *Lady Windermere's Fan*, *An Ideal Husband*, *Salome*, *De Profundis* (on his downfall), and numerous memorable fairy tales, including the decidedly Christian tale, "The Selfish Giant."

3. SEAN O'CASEY

Born John Casey in 1884 in Dublin into a working-class Protestant family, O'Casey was active in the Irish nationalist and socialist movements in his early years before becoming disenchanted with politics in general and moving to London. After initially showcasing his work through the Abbey Theatre, O'Casey experienced hard feelings over a rejection that led to more of his work performed in England and the United States than on the Emerald Isle. The 1958 withdrawal of his play, *The Drums of Father Ned*, because of clerical concerns led him to forbid all productions of his work in Ireland until after his own death.

Among his major works are *The Shadow of a Gunman*, *Juno and the Paycock*, *The Plough and the Stars*, and *The Silver Tassie*.

4.   J. M. SYNGE

Born John Millington Synge in Rathfarnham, County Dublin, in 1871 to very religious parents, Synge became a key figure in the secular literary revival with his ear for dialect and his understanding of classical themes, prose, and poetry. Although there was some ambivalence toward his works in terms of nationalism and religion, he was considered by both sides of each issue to be a major influence on early twentieth-century Irish literature.

Among his major works are *The Playboy of the Western World*, *In the Shadow of the Glen*, and *Riders to the Sea*.

5.   JONATHAN SWIFT

Anglican cleric born in Dublin in 1667, Dean Swift was more than just the author of *Gulliver's Travels*; he was perhaps the greatest prose satirist ever to come out of Ireland. Essays, letter, parodies, and pamphlets—he did it all with panache and a bitter wit, despite his Church of England affiliation.

Among his major works are *A Tale of a Tub*, *Drapier's Letters*, "A Modest Proposal" (an essay in which he proposed consuming the children of Ireland to deal with the population explosion and famine at the same time), and *The Battle of the Books*.

6. RICHARD BRINSLEY SHERIDAN

Born in Dublin in 1751, playwright Sheridan is credited with coining the often misused term, "malapropism." He abandoned his life in the theater (though not necessarily his final interest therein) in 1780, when he became a member of Parliament, and, as a result, ended his life in poverty and shame with the loss of his parliamentary seat, fortune, and sanity.

Among his major works are *The Rivals*, *The School for Scandal*, and *The Critic*.

7. SEAMUS HEANEY

Born in Derry in 1939, Heaney, as well as others in the Belfast poet's circle, molded powerful verses to convey their feelings about the Northern Ireland political situation and the cultural heritage of the Irish people as a single nation.

Among Heaney's most famous works are *Death of a Naturalist*, *The Haw Lantern*, *The Spirit Level*, and *Beowulf: A New Translation*, the last of which has the distinction of being the first time that this classic epic of yesterday made an appearance on the *New York Times*' hardcover best-sellers list. He was awarded the Nobel Prize for Literature in 1995.

8. GEORGE BERNARD SHAW

Born in Dublin in 1856, Shaw left the Emerald Isle at age twenty to pursue work in London as a theater critic. He gradually expanded the focus of his criticism and rejoiced in skewering all manner of subjects and society, usually not caring whom or what he might be offending. Oscar Wilde related it best: "he [Shaw] hasn't an enemy in the world, but unfortunately none of his friends like him." Shaw was particularly adept at social commentary in his columns and, more important, in his plays. Indeed, one might read all of his works to gain a metaphoric encapsulation of the downfall of the British Empire in the twentieth century.

Among his most famous works are *Arms and the Man*, *Mrs. Warren's Profession* (dealing with the subject of integrity and prostitution, both Shavian favorites), *Man and Superman* (featuring "Don Juan in Hell"), *Pygmalion* (the basis for the hit musical, *My Fair Lady*), and *Heartbreak House*.

9. SAMUEL BECKETT

Born in Foxrock outside of Dublin in 1906 and educated at Trinity College, Beckett moved to France, where he quickly became part of James Joyce's circle and established himself as a bilingual playwright and poet. He received the Croix de Guerre for his service in the French Resistance before and during World War II.

His most famous works are *Waiting for Godot*, *Endgame*, *Happy Days*, and the poem, "Whoroscope."

10. JOHN KEYES BYRNE

Born in Dublin in 1926 and raised in Dalkey, Byrne worked in the civil service until achieving success in the theater under the pseudonym, Hugh Leonard (the name of the protagonist in one of his first rejected works). Much of his work is semiautobiographical.

Among Byrne's major works are *Da* (which was also filmed with Barnard Hughes, reprising his Tony Award winning Broadway performance), *A Life* (which features the character of Drum, who first appeared in *Da*), and *Time Was*.

Pearls of Wisdom from Oscar Wilde

Gentleman, philosopher, literary wonder, and decadent dilettante, the immortal Oscar Wilde always had a way with words and was more than willing to share his views with anyone sufficiently thick-skinned and fast enough on the uptake to handle his rapier wit.

1. YOUTH

Alternately credited to both Oscar Wilde and George Bernard Shaw: "Youth is wasted on the young" laments the joy of youth being wasted on those too young to know what to do with it. Similarly, Wilde is also quoted as saying, "I am not young enough to know everything."

2. TEMPTATION

Of temptation, Wilde wrote in *The Picture of Dorian Gray*, "I can resist everything except temptation," and "The only way to get rid of a temptation is to yield to it."

3. BEING TALKED ABOUT

As Wilde put it in *The Picture of Dorian Gray*, "There is only one thing in the world worse than being talked about, and that is not being talked about."

4. CYNICISM

"A cynic is a man who knows the price of everything and the value of nothing."

5. MARTYRDOM

Per Wilde, "A thing is not necessarily true because a man dies for it."

6. THE TRUTH

"The truth is rarely pure, and never simple."

7. WAR

From Wilde's *The Critic as Artist*: "As long as war is regarded as wicked, it will always have its fascination. When it is looked upon as vulgar, it will cease to be popular."

8. SOCIETY

"Never speak disrespectfully of society. Only people who can't get into it do that." So said Oscar Wilde in *The Importance of Being Earnest*.

9. ENEMIES

Also from *The Picture of Dorian Gray*: "A man cannot be too careful in the choice of his enemies," Wilde also suggests, "Always forgive your enemies. Nothing annoys them so much."

Oscar Wilde

10. **LOOKING UP**

In *Lady Windermere's Fan*, Wilde writes, "We are all in the gutter, but some of us are looking at the stars."

Actors of the Emerald Isle

The hard-drinking, rowdy, and reckless Irish actor always ready for a fight or a frolic is more than a stereotype—it is an archetype, and, on more than one occasion, it is very accurate. The fact that these thespians can act your socks off sober or not is also true, leaving the Emerald Isle with a talent pool the rest of the world would be surely jealous of.

1. PETER O'TOOLE

Born in Connemara in 1932, Peter O'Toole is one of the world's most lauded film actors. Still going strong in a great diversity of roles though he is now in his seventies, O'Toole has received Academy Award nominations for a wide array of parts, ranging from comic to historical, from gentleman noble to scary psychotic.

He made his feature film debut in Walt Disney's production of Robert Louis Stevenson's *Kidnapped* in which he dueled in bagpipes with leading man Peter Finch. His multivolume-in-progress memoir is entitled, *Loitering with Intent.*

Among O'Toole's major films are *Lawrence of Arabia* (for which he was nominated for an Academy Award); *Beckett* and *The Lion in Winter* (playing the same character of Henry II at different stages in his life for both of which he received an Academy Award nomination); *The Ruling Class* (playing a mad noble of England who fancies himself to be Jesus Christ but is cured of his insanity when he believes that he is really Jack the Ripper); *Caligula* (in which he played a pedophiliac Emperor Tiberius); *My Favorite Year*; *High Spirits* (filmed in Ireland); and *The Last Emperor* (for which he received his first Oscar nomination in the Supporting Actor category). His most recent film appearance was in *Troy*.

In 2004 O'Toole received an honorary Academy Award—his first actual Oscar despite all of his nominations.

2. **BARRY FITZGERALD**

Born William Joseph Shields in Dublin in 1888, Fitzgerald has the distinction of having been a childhood acquaintance of James Joyce and a temporary roommate of Sean O'Casey (for whom it is rumored that O'Casey wrote *The Silver Tassie*) before moving to Hollywood as a contract player to recreate a role he originated on the stage for the 1936 film version of *The Plough and the Stars*. He is also the only actor in Academy Award history to win the Oscar for a part for which he was nominated as both Best Actor and Best Supporting Actor.

Among his major films are *How Green Was My Valley*, *The Quiet Man*, *Going My Way* (his Academy Award–winning role), *The Story of Seabiscuit*, and *The Naked City*.

3. KENNETH BRANAGH

Born in Belfast in 1960, Branagh is recognized as the Laurence Olivier of his generation through his mastery of Shakespeare on film and the versatility and virtuosity of his performances in myriad roles, many of which he masters both in front of (as actor) and behind the camera (as director) simultaneously. Branagh has also brought a certain amount of balance to his repertoire, with numerous supporting roles in more commercial ventures.

Among his major films (as an actor) are *Henry V*, *Hamlet* (set in Romanov-era Russia), *Dead Again*, *Swing Kids*, *Mary Shelley's Frankenstein*, *Celebrity* (directed by Woody Allen), and *The Road to El Dorado* (voice).

4. RICHARD HARRIS

Born in Limerick in 1932, Harris played numerous military "spear carriers" in such films as *Shake Hands with the Devil*, *The Wreck of the Mary Deare*, and *The Guns of Navarone* before achieving critical stardom with his portrayal of a North of England Rugby player in *This Sporting Life*, which led to his being offered and accepting a number of Richard Burton's cast-off roles, along with some of the star turn excesses that went with the territory. Older and wiser and out of detox, Harris reclaimed his prominence in the field with several Academy Award nominations late in his career.

He is also a notable one-hit wonder in the music business for his rendition of "MacArthur's Park."

Among Harris's major films are *Camelot* (in the Richard Burton Broadway role of King Arthur), *The Molly Maguires* (opposite Sean Connery), *A Man Called Horse* (opposite Dame Judith Anderson),

Cromwell (opposite Sir Alec Guinness), *The Field* (for which he was nominated for an Academy Award), *Unforgiven* (in which he played English Bob, a British gunman in the Old West), and *Gladiator*.

5. STEPHEN BOYD

Born in Belfast in 1928, Boyd definitely falls into the I-never-thought-of-him-as-being-Irish category. He hit Hollywood as a cross between Rod Taylor and Charlton Heston but never managed to be more than a pretty-face leading man.

His major films include *Ben Hur* (opposite Charlton Heston in the title role), *The Fall of the Roman Empire*, *Fantastic Voyage*, *Billy Rose's Jumbo*, and *Hannie Calder* (in which he reteamed with Raquel Welch from *Fantastic Voyage*).

6. CYRIL CUSACK

Strictly speaking, Cusack was born in South Africa in 1910, but his many years spent living in Ireland and working on the Irish stage more than qualify him for this list. Indeed, he is the spiritual patriarch of many actors who have come through the Dublin and Abbey theaters.

Among Cusack's films are *Odd Man Out*, *The Spy Who Came in from the Cold*, *Fahrenheit 451*, *My Left Foot*, and *Far and Away*.

7. COLIN FARRELL

The Irish "It Boy" of the moment, Farrell was born in Dublin in 1976 and attended Gaiety School of Acting. He attracted attention while still in his teens when he landed the role of Danny in the TV series, *Bally-kissangel*. From there the stage and then Hollywood beckoned as he makes way toward stardom.

His major films include *Tigerland*, *Hart's War*, *Daredevil*, *Minority Report*, *Phone Booth*, and *Alexander the Great*.

8. STEPHEN REA

Born in Belfast in 1946, Rea had much theater and TV experience before becoming noticed in Neil Jordan's films, one of which (*The Crying Game*) led to his nomination for an Academy Award for Best Actor. Despite his screen success he often returns to TV/cable roles (as in HBO's *Citizen X* and *The Crime of the Century*) and the stage.

Among his major film roles are *The Doctor and the Devils*, *Michael Collins* (also directed by Neil Jordan), *The Butcher Boy*, and *Prêt-à-Porter* (*Ready to Wear*).

9. GABRIEL BYRNE

Born in Dublin in 1950, Byrne trained for the stage and plied his craft with the Dublin Shakespeare Society and the Abbey Theatre. His early work in television led to critical notice on the BBC leading to a major part in the film, *Defence of the Realm*.

Among Byrne's major film roles are *Gothic* (as Lord Byron), *Miller's Crossing*, *Little Women*, *The Usual Suspects*, and *End of Days* (as Satan).

10. PIERCE BROSNAN

Born in 1952 in County Meath, Brosnan studied acting in England before landing his first film role as an unnamed Irish Republican Army gunman in *The Long Goodbye*, which led to a starring role in the U.S. mini-series, *The Manions of America*, and the lead in the hit romantic mystery series, *Remington Steele*. He was offered the role of James Bond in 1986 but lost out to

Timothy Dalton for two films due to a contractual conflict in scheduling before finally assaying the role of
Agent 007 in *GoldenEye* in 1995.

Among his major non-Bond film roles are *The
Fourth Protocol*, *Mrs. Doubtfire*, *The Nephew*, and *The
Thomas Crown Affair* (where he filled the role played
previously by Steve McQueen).

Irish Actresses

On stage and screen Irish lasses have plied their trade the world over, and when leading ladies were sought in Hollywood, the Emerald Isle was a breeding ground for quality. The young colleens traded in the Abbey Theatre for the Old West, and Shakespeare and O'Casey for playing second fiddle to a verbally impaired Olympic swimmer and his chimp sidekick.

1. SARAH ALLGOOD

Born in Dublin in 1883, Allgood appeared in early stage productions of Lady Gregory's *Spreading the News* and J. M. Synge's *Playboy of the Western World*. She moved to Hollywood in the late thirties, and appeared in well over thirty American films.

Among her movies are *Juno and the Paycock*, *Blackmail* (directed by Alfred Hitchcock), *Jane Eyre*, *The Lodger* (directed by Alfred Hitchcock), and *Cheaper by the Dozen*.

2. RIA MOONEY

Born in 1903 in Dublin, Mooney made her stage debut at the age of six and later won acclaim for her performance in *The Plough and the Stars*. She was the first woman director of the Abbey Theatre (1948—1963) and also served with Dublin's Gate Theatre and London's Peacock Theatre.

3. SIOBHAN MCKENNA

Born in Belfast in 1923 and reared in Galway, McKenna made her professional acting debut in an Irish-language production. In 1944 she joined the Abbey Theatre company and has since received numerous honors for her stage work.

Among her films are *King of Kings*, *Playboy of the Western World*, and *Doctor Zhivago*.

4. MAUREEN O'HARA

Born Maureen FitzSimons in Dublin in 1920, O'Hara started her thespian career on the radio while still a child, then trained with the Abbey Players as a teenager before moving on to films. She arrived in Hollywood in the late 1930s, where she debuted as Esmeralda to Charles Laughton's Quasimodo in *The Hunchback of Notre Dame*. She was one of John Ford's favorite leading ladies, an aptly cast romantic foil for John Wayne.

Among her films are *How Green Was My Valley*, *The Quiet Man* (opposite John Wayne), *Jamaica Inn* (directed by Alfred Hitchcock), *The Parent Trap* (for Walt Disney), and *Big Jake* (once again, opposite John Wayne).

5. MAUREEN O'SULLIVAN

Born in Boyle, County Roscommon, in 1911, O'Sullivan was discovered by American director Frank Borzage in Dublin in 1929 while she was preparing for a part in Ireland's first talkie, *Song o' My Heart*.

Most familiar to today's audiences as Jane to Johnny Weissmuller's Tarzan and the mother of Mia Farrow, O'Sullivan starred in *Tarzan the Ape Man* and a number of its sequels, *David Copperfield*, *The Big Clock* (opposite Ray Milland and Charles Laughton and later remade in the 1980s as *No Way Out* with Sean Young, Kevin Costner, and Gene Hackman), and *Hannah and Her Sisters* (directed by Woody Allen).

6. GREER GARSON

Born in County Down in 1908, Garson was educated in London, working in theater as a hobby until she was offered a place in a repertory company, which eventually led to acclaim on the London stage. Her work caught the eye of Louis B. Mayer, who lured her to Hollywood with an MGM contract that made her one of America's most popular leading ladies.

Among her films are *Goodbye, Mr. Chips*, *Mrs. Miniver* (for which she received an Academy Award for Best Actress), *Madame Curie*, *Sunrise at Campobello*, and *Little Women*.

7. ROMA DOWNEY

Born in 1960s County Derry, Downey witnessed the Troubles as a Roman Catholic in Northern Ireland and was present at the events of "Bloody Sunday" on January 30, 1972. She received her theatrical training at London Drama Studio, and in 1989 she was cast in

Rex Harrison's Broadway production of *The Circle*, which led to her landing her first TV role as Jacqueline Kennedy in the mini-series, *A Woman Named Jackie*. Other roles followed, and she landed the part of everyone's favorite angel, Monica, in the cult favorite, feel-good TV series, *Touched by an Angel*.

Among her TV films are *Devlin*, *Hercules and the Amazonian Women*, *The Last Word*, *A Hairy Tale*, and *The Survivors' Club*.

8. BRENDA FRICKER

Born in Dublin in 1945, Fricker cut her teeth in regional Irish theater before moving on to the National Theatre and the Royal Shakespeare Company. She was first noticed by American audiences in her Academy Award–winning performance as Christy Brown's mother.

Among her films are *My Left Foot* (for which she received an Academy Award as Best Supporting Actress), *The Field*, *So I Married an Axe Murderer*, *A Man of No Importance*, and *A Time to Kill*.

9. UNA O'CONNOR

Born in 1880, this accomplished actress is primarily remembered for her semi-comic-relief roles as a screaming eye witness/maid/villager in numerous horror and murder mysteries. Among O'Connor's films are *The Invisible Man* (where she played a screaming woman), *The Informer*, *The Bride of Frankenstein* (where she played a screaming woman), *The Canterville Ghost* (where she played—can you guess?—a screaming woman), and *Witness for the Prosecution* (her last role, nonscreaming or otherwise).

10. **GERALDINE FITZGERALD**

Born in Dublin in 1914, this grand dame of the American cinema has had a career that spanned the century, from the mid-thirties to the late eighties with time out for TV and stage roles. Among her films are *Wuthering Heights*, *Dark Victory*, *The Pawnbroker*, *The Last American Hero*, *Harry and Tonto*, and *Arthur*.

Out-of-Place Irish

The so-called Irish Diaspora has led to all things Irish turning up in the darnedest places. Though the fruits and favors of the Emerald Isle are now enjoyed all over the world, sometimes some of these appearances have seemed to be a bit out of place or at least unexpected.

1. **DUCK, YOU SUCKER (AKA *A FISTFUL OF DYNAMITE*) (1972)**

A true smorgasbord of filmmaking. In this minor classic spaghetti western directed by Sergio Leone, James Coburn plays an IRA demolition expert—complete with Irish brogue—lending mercenary support to a two-bit Mexican bandit (played by Rod Steiger) who gets swept up in a revolution.

Leone masterfully uses flashbacks of Coburn's experiences in Ireland to thematically link all revolutions, especially with reference to betrayal.

Although Leone had expertly dubbed from Italian to Spanish and English (and back again) in the past with such international hits as *The Good, the Bad, and the Ugly*, one can only wonder how Coburn's brogue sounded in Italian.

2. *LEPRECHAUN 5: IN THE HOOD* (1999)

Warwick Davis (of *Ewok* and *Willow* fame) reprised his role as the leprechaun from hell out to reclaim his gold in the fifth film of this eponymous series in which he bedevils some homeys and rampages with rap stars (including Ice-T) as the film franchise sank to new lows in a silly attempt to rip off the once successful black exploitation film genre that twenty-five years ago produced such classics as *Blacula* and *Dr. Jekyll and Mr. Black*.

3. *FINIAN'S RAINBOW* (1947 BROADWAY MUSICAL/ 1968 FILM)

When you want to tell a fairy-tale story of American racism, what better way to do it than by using as your focal character a ne'er-do-well Irishman (Finian) being pursued by a leprechaun in search of his stolen gold. The Broadway musical was preachy, and the 1968 film with Fred Astaire not even attempting an accent was even worse. It's hard to believe the film was directed by Francis Ford Coppola, which, of course, brings us to . . .

4. *THE GODFATHER* BY MARIO PUZO

At any Corleone family get-together, one can't help but notice red-haired Tom Hagen, the family con-sigliore, and wonder, what's a nice Irish kid like him doing with a real "Family" family.

As explained in both the book and the movie, Tom was a friend of Sonny's whom the family adopted away from his abusive father. He was as much a member of the family as a non-Italian could be, but by the third and weakest film of the series, he had left the family business and entered the priesthood, thus opting out of appearing in the film.

5. *SCARLETT: THE SEQUEL TO GONE WITH THE WIND* BY ALEXANDRA RIPLEY

When the Margaret Mitchell estate authorized Ripley to write the sequel to the classic Confederate romance of a genteel South that probably never existed, were readers really ready for the quick skip across the pond to the Emerald Isle that takes up so much of the sequel?

Perhaps it was Alex Haley who inspired Ripley to seek Scarlett's roots from the pre-Civil War era?

6. *THE MISSOURI BREAKS* (1976)

With a screenplay by Thomas McGuane, direction by Arthur Penn, and two recent Academy Award winners headlining, this film was not expected to be a run-of-the-mill western, but Marlon Brando's starring stint as an obese and deadly Irish regulator with an occasional penchant for drag stands out as much as John Wayne's portrayal of Genghis Khan in *The Conqueror* and Alec Guinness's turn as a Haitian woman in *The Comedians.*

7. AMBROSE BERNARD O'HIGGINS (1720-1810)

When one studies the great figures of Spanish history or the settlement/colonization of South America, it's fairly safe to say that one does not necessarily expect to come across a favored son of the Emerald Isle, but such is the case with Ambrose Bernard O'Higgins.

O'Higgins was born in County Meath, Ireland; educated in Cadiz, Spain; and moved to South America, where he initially worked as a peddler before joining the Spanish Army and finally ending up as Viceroy of Peru, the highest rank in the Spanish colonial service. Not bad for a kid from County Meath.

8. JAMES JOYCE'S *ULYSSES* (1922)

Considered by many critics to be the greatest twentieth-century novel of Ireland (if not the English language), the novel traces the actions of its characters during a single day in Dublin. Unfortunately, this great Irish novel by the greatest-ever Irish writer was not originally published in Ireland or in any English-speaking country; it was published in France, having been banned for obscenity by the ancestral country that now claims it among its national treasures.

9. *STAR TREK—THE NEXT GENERATION* AND *STAR TREK—DEEP SPACE NINE*

It must be written somewhere in the Starfleet manuals that a British Isles' accent is required to run the transporter. The original series had its Scotty (played by James Doohan) and its first two spin-offs had O'Brien (played by Colm Meaney).

It's amazing that in an enlightened future of multicultural diversity, as promised by Roddenberry's universe, the only stereotype to survive is the hard-drinking Irishman, always ready for a fight or a frolic. In space no one can hear your brogue, which of course brings us to . . .

10. *LEPRECHAUN 4: IN SPACE* (1996)

'Nuff said. Not since the Space Family Robinson had to deal with an outer space leprechaun on the sixties

TV series, *Lost in Space*, has there been such a blarney-filled attempt at a science fiction crossover. Though the space marines arrive to save the day, nothing can save moviegoers from this low point in the *Leprechaun* franchise. It should probably be mentioned here that Warwick Davis has appeared as a leprechaun in numerous non-*Leprechaun* films, most of which are substantially better than any of the films in this franchise.

U.S. Film Appearances by Irish Republican Army Members

Hollywood has had an easy time in the past passing IRA terrorists and exiles through immigration into the United States faster than you can say the Department of Homeland Security. Sometimes they're here for fund-raising, other times for assassinations, and sometimes just to have a little fun and try to fit in. Nothing obvious seems to give them away, not even the fact that as usual not all of their accents are convincing. I guess no one ever heard of IRA profiling.

1. JEFF BRIDGES (AS JIMMY DOVE/LIAM MCGIVNEY) IN *BLOWN AWAY* (1994)

Boston Police Department bomb disposal expert has a slight secret in his past—he was formerly a member of the IRA. I guess the police department doesn't bother to do background checks on immigrants, let alone applicants with specialized knowledge.

2. **TOMMY LEE JONES (AS RYAN GAERITY) IN *BLOWN AWAY* (1994)**

Jimmy/Liam's old friend has broken out of prison and now wants revenge . . . which makes you wonder: if he was such a master terrorist in the first place that he's now able to elude an international dragnet, how did they ever manage to catch him in the first place? Still, it's a treat to see Jones doing his demolition dance to the chords of U2.

3. **SEAN BEAN (AS SEAN MILLER) IN *PATRIOT GAMES* (1992)**

Though the moviemakers went to great pains in their adaptation of the Tom Clancy novel to specifically reference Miller's affiliation with a radical and disowned faction of the IRA—so the audience knows he's a really bad terrorist rather than a misunderstood freedom fighter—he is nonetheless able to get close enough to kill a presidential aide as well as a member of the English royal family.

4. **STEPHEN REA (AS DOWD) IN *THE BREAK* (1997)**

Though Stephen Rea is probably best known for his portrayal of a different IRA rebel in *The Crying Game*, his again disillusioned (though this time not sexually confused) gunman by the name of Dowd breaks out of prison in Britain and manages to escape to New York, only to travel south to Guatemala, where he gets involved with rebellions of another kind with a little help from the North American Free Trade Agreement (NAFTA).

5. **BRAD PITT (AS RORY DEVANEY) IN** *THE DEVIL'S OWN* **(1997)**

The nice kid from Ireland who is taken under the wing by a streetwise New York cop (played by Harrison Ford) turns out to be a ten-most-wanted IRA hit man, which doesn't really say much about the street smarts of the cop.

6. **RICHARD GERE (AS DECLAN MULQUEEN) IN** *THE JACKAL* **(1997)**

Very loosely based on the Frederick Forsyth novel, *The Day of the Jackal* (which didn't have any IRA characters in it and took place in France), *Jackal* reimagines the story, sets it in America, and, in a truly subversive moment, makes an IRA rebel the hero (a part that in the original was assigned to a Columbo-like French cop) in the plot to foil a super-assassin with an unknown quarry.

Gere's accent, and his role, for that matter, are gratuitous at best.

7. **SEAN "RUSTY" REGAN IN** *THE BIG SLEEP* **(1946)**

Though this character never appears on screen in Howard Hawks's marvelous film adaptation of Raymond Chandler's novel, he is the object of Marlowe's investigation, General Sternwood's bodyguard, and close companion who commanded an IRA brigade.

8. **STERLING HAYDEN (AS SEAMUS FLAHERTY) IN** *THE OUTSIDER* **(1979)**

Idealistic American Vietnam vet (Craig Wasson) tries to follow in his kindly old grandfather's (Hayden) footsteps by traveling to Ireland to join the IRA, only to suffer disillusionment similar to that which he experienced in Vietnam.

9. CLIVE REVILL (AS JOE DEVLIN) IN *COLUMBO— THE CONSPIRATORS* (1978)

Likeable poet and raconteur Devlin (a sort of combination Seamus Heaney and Malachy McCourt) runs guns for the IRA while touring for his publisher. Only when he dispatches a traitor/blackmailer does anyone, and then only the rumpled Lt. Columbo (Peter Falk), bother to check into his easily suspicious background.

Note: A similar argument can be used concerning Richard Harris's character in *Patriot Games*, but perhaps hiding in plain sight as an IRA fund-raiser in the United States is enough of a cover.

10. LIAM DEVLIN AND SEAN DILLON IN THE NOVELS OF JACK HIGGINS

Since Devlin's first appearance in *The Eagle Has Landed*, it has become quite apparent that Higgins has considerable amount of affection for the über IRA gunman despite the fact that he conspired with the Nazis in an attempt to kidnap Churchill, so much in fact that he just had to bring him back in subsequent novels, keeping him preternaturally active well into his eighties.

Dillon, Higgins's slightly more politically correct and definitely younger successor to Devlin (who has both opposed and joined forces with him on different occasions), shares the IRA rap sheet but is definitely more inclined to work with nonterrorist establishments . . . which still never answers the question of how such wanted men can come and go in the United States with such ease.

Cinematic Masterpieces of the Old Sod

Not all Irish movies deal with the Irish Republican Army, though it is probably fair to say that all Irish films do deal with the troubles of the Irish people. Given the rich history and lore, family and faith, spirits and the spirited, it's only fitting that Irish cinema is as varied as the colors in a leprechaun's rainbow or the shades of green in attendance at a St. Patty's Day parade.

1. *MICHAEL COLLINS* (1996) DIRECTED BY NEIL JORDAN

Quite literally, this is the *Lawrence of Arabia* of the Emerald Isle, a truly marvelous historical epic of the tumultuous times between the Rising and the Irish Civil War as told through the story of the "big fella" and father of the IRA, Michael Collins.

True, Julia Roberts does lose her accent enough times to make this film the basis of a drinking game, but Alan Rickman, Stephen Rea, Aidan Quinn, and Liam Neeson more than make up for it with wonderfully nuanced performances that clearly differentiate the rebels as individuals and not just a bunch of IRA gunman or saintly saviors of the Emerald Isle.

2. *THE DEAD* (1987) DIRECTED BY JOHN HUSTON

Like the James Joyce novella on which it is based, this is ostensibly the story of a Christmas get-together where the metaphoric ghosts of the past in the form of regrets and disappointments dampen the spirits of the holiday season. Peopled with familiar faces, from the relative who has fallen off the wagon even though he had agreed "to take the pledge for the holidays," to the dutiful dowager, the boisterous master, and the couple who realize that love has left their lives, this film is ripe with masterful performances by Angelica Huston, Dan O'Herlihy, and Donal McCann.

This is quite possibly the best cinematic adaptation of any of Joyce's works as well as possibly John Huston's finest film. Sadly it was also his last.

3. *MAN OF ARAN* (1934) DIRECTED BY ROBERT FLAHERTY

This documentary by the famous filmmaker who also did *Nanook of the North* took three years to make, as Flaherty painstakingly documented the day-to-day struggles of a fisherman on the Aran Islands, three limestone isles located in Galway Bay on the west coast of the Republic of Ireland.

4. *DARBY O'GILL AND THE LITTLE PEOPLE* (1959) DIRECTED BY ROBERT STEVENSON

One of the two of Walt Disney's Irish projects (the other was *The Fighting Prince of Donegal*), this magical adaptation of the story of an old codger who encounter Brian Connors, the Leprechaun King (from the stories by Herminie T. Kavanagh) is a marvelous mix of Emerald Isle enchantment and malevolence that also boasts the acting and singing film debut of a Scottish actor by the name of Sean Connery.

5. ***BROKEN HARVEST* (1994) DIRECTED BY MAURICE O'CALLAGHAN**

Based on O'Callaghan's own story, "The Shilling," this is a marvelous tale of 1950s Cork when a failed wheat harvest leads to hardened feelings from the past between two rebels from the Rising who parted ways and allegiances during the Civil War, that now threaten to destroy them both. This film features the artful use of black and white interspersed with the color story-telling and terrifically captured scenes of the Irish landscape.

6. ***THE BRYLCREEM BOYS* (1996) DIRECTED BY TERENCE RYAN**

This film is memorable primarily because of its backdrop—the World War II years of open Irish neutrality, when Allied and Axis soldiers alike were held as POWs to avoid the republic having to take sides in the conflict. As depicted here in classic Hollywood fashion, imprisonment conditions were far from oppressive, with all credibility further undercut by the story of both Axis and Allied prisoners vying for the same girl while also trying to escape so that they can return to the fighting.

7. ***THE FIELD* (1990) DIRECTED BY JIM SHERIDAN**

Ostensibly, this is the simple story of an old tenant farmer (played by Academy Award–nominated Richard Harris) who is forced to confront changing times when it appears that the land he has tended all of his life is going to be sold to an American developer. The sale will leave him with nothing to show for his lifetime of toil. Obviously it's all a metaphor for the history of the Irish Free State, but it's also a really good movie in its own right.

8. *FaR anD away* (1992) DIRECTED BY RON HOWARD

Panoramic, unlikely love story of haves and have-nots who emigrate to America from Ireland, this film manages to move from the Emerald Isle's agrarian fields of green to the decadent city ports of East Coast America and on to the fresh frontier of the American West, where everyone is entitled to a new beginning. Tom Cruise and Nicole Kidman met and fell in love during filming, and even though it's very sloppily sentimental à la Hollywood in the thirties and forties, the early parts in Ireland are marvelously earthy.

9. *In THE naME OF THE FaTHER* (1993) DIRECTED BY JIM SHERIDAN

This is the story of one of the great miscarriages of justice in the Crown's dealings with Ireland in modern times, in which Daniel Day-Lewis plays Gerry Conlin who, along with his infirm father, was convicted in connection to an IRA bombing on the basis of trumped-up charges, concealed exculpatory evidence, and undue political influence. In addition to being a serious exposé of British injustice during the modern Troubles, the film also fashions a meaningful story of a boy and his "da" who are at odds with each due to the tumultuousness of the times.

10. *THE COMMITMEnTS* (1991) DIRECTED BY ALAN PARKER

Soul music comes to Dublin as an enterprising young lad forms a rhythm and blues band to invigorate the working masses of the inner city. Full of memorable characters and toe-tapping new renditions of classic R&B standards like "Mustang Sally" and "Try a Little Tenderness," the film brings the same electric enthusiasm to Parker's subject matter that the director achieved earlier in his career with *Fame*.

Based on the Roddy Doyle novel of the same name, it is worth noting that the other two books (*The Snapper* and *The Van*) in this trilogy were also made into films with Colm Meaney playing the same part in each one.

Irish Filmmakers

The Irish film industry, and its Emerald Isle talent behind the camera, has finally managed to distinguish itself as a separate branch of world cinema from its British brethren.

Though these directors thrive on materials that reflect their heritage and the issues of the world around them, their dedication to the craft of filmmaking has made their works far from parochial and, indeed, well deserving of the wide-ranging international audiences they now enjoy.

1. NEIL JORDAN

Born in Sligo in 1950, screenwriter/director Jordan has won an Academy Award for screenwriting and is the most commercially successful Irish director in the business today, with a number films to his credit. His work delves into the Irish tradition and the dark fantastic as well as, occasionally, edgier, more contemporary takes on these themes.

Among his films are *Mona Lisa*, *The Company of Wolves* (featuring Stephen Rea), *The Crying Game* (for which he won a screenwriting Academy Award; it also stars Stephen Rea), *Michael Collins* (featuring Stephen Rea), *High Spirits*, and *Interview with the Vampire* (based on the Anne Rice novel, and, of course, also featuring Stephen Rea).

2. JIM SHERIDAN

Born in Dublin in 1949, Sheridan started his career as a playwright turned screenwriter studying film at New York University. Working for many years to get backing for his cinematic adaptation of the life of Christy Brown, Sheridan finally got the chance to direct the film himself. That and his next two films earned a total of thirteen Academy Award nominations.

Not surprising, the Irish experience is usually the focus of his work. Among his films are *My Left Foot*, *The Field*, *In the Name of the Father*, and *In America*, all of which have earned Academy Award nominations.

3. KENNETH BRANAGH

Born in Belfast in 1960, Branagh has seized the moniker of Ireland's Olivier with his critically acclaimed direction of five cinematic versions of Shakespeare's plays, ranging from an Olivier homage in Shakespearean literacy, to a classic transposed to Imperial Russia, to a romp set to the music of Cole Porter.

He has fearlessly explored other avenues as well and has proven himself to be a directorial master of the contemporary thriller. Among his films are *Henry V*, *Dead Again*, *Much Ado About Nothing*, *Hamlet*, and *Love's Labour's Lost*.

4. CATHAL BLACK

Born in 1952, Black has embraced an extremely edgy sensibility that he conveys in contemporary Irish cinema and, indeed, has experienced a certain backlash among more traditional audiences due to his portrayals of gay themes and the darker side of Catholic education. Among his films are *Wheels*, *Our Boys*, *Pigs*, and *Love and Rage*.

5. DONALD BLACK

Born in 1951, Black is considered to be Ireland's leading contemporary documentary filmmaker. His work has covered the gauntlet of subjects in Ireland from sports to politics to pathology. Among his films are *At the Cinema Place*, *The Joy*, *Hearts and Souls*, and *Dead Man's Doctor*.

6. PIERCE BROSNAN

Though primarily known as an actor, this Drogheda-born leading man recently embarked on a second career as a director and producer and has acquitted himself in a manner that would make the Emerald Isle proud.

The film, *Evelyn*, tells the story of a man who must fight the system to regain custody of his children from the Catholic Church–run orphanages to which the courts have consigned them. Brosnan has assembled an accomplished cast, including Stephen Rea, Aidan Quinn, Alan Bates, and Julianna Margulies, in a heartfelt film that dares to question the traditional Irish church-state alliance.

Another of his contemporary Irish films is *The Nephew*, which deals with racial tension in the old sod.

7. **PAT MURPHY**

Born in Dublin in 1951, Murphy is primarily regarded as a critically acclaimed director solely on the basis of three films in a span of twenty years, all dealing with feminism in Ireland. They range from the hidden history of the women of the rebellion of 1803 to the story of the relationship between James Joyce and Nora Barnacle. Her films are *Maeve*, *Anna Devlin*, and *Nora*.

8. **ENDE HUGHES**

A leading light in the new wave of Northern Ireland filmmaking, Hughes has embraced a pop sensibility with commercially themed films that nonetheless bring the political realities of the North to the silver screen. His most famous films are *The Eliminator* and *Flying Saucer Rock 'n' Roll*.

9. **DAVID CAFFREY**

Another relative newcomer from the North, Caffrey has directed numerous shorts, and in 1998 he directed his first feature, the well-received *Divorcing Jack*, from the novel by Colin Bateman.

10. **JOHN HUSTON**

Though unmistakably American, Huston spent a great deal of his professional life living in Ireland. He shot *The List of Adrian Messenger* there, did the preproduction work and script consultation for *Moby Dick* there, and spent a great deal of his own leisure time carousing there in a manner befitting a wealthy Irish country gentleman. Indeed, Ray Bradbury, the scriptwriter for *Moby Dick*, based a character on Huston in his short story, "The Banshee"; evidently everything in the story but that which was supernatural was taken from Bradbury's memories of those tumultuous meetings.

Huston's last film, a collaboration with his son and daughter, was filmed there as well—the very success-ful film version of James Joyce's novella, *The Dead*.

Acts, Shows, and Entertainers

From local pub acts to Broadway-caliber shows to sell-out arena concerts, Irish entertainment has never been more popular or diverse. Whether it's bold and contemporary, with an edgy flash, or sentimentally nostalgic, with a tenor's tenor or an instrumental melody, Irish entertainment can be found at numerous venues year-round. It's not just for St. Patrick's Day parties any more.

1. THE IRISH TENORS

Combining the marketing hooks of "The Three Tenors" with *Riverdance*, the Irish Tenors are three classically trained performers with strong voices, a lot of enthusiasm, and more than a bit of whimsy. John McDermott (later replaced by Finbar Wright, due to a death in the family), Anthony Kearns, and Ronan Tynan appear together on a small, plain stage and sing mostly traditional songs—She Moved Through the Fair," "Will Ye Go, Lassie, Go?"—in both solos and trios with a full orchestra in front of an appreciative audience.

Their records go platinum, their concerts sell out, and their TV specials are hits all over the world, guaranteeing each a successful solo career as well. Note that the success of the Irish Tenors has led to the formation of several other trios with confusing monikers such as "The Three Irish Tenors" and "The Three Tenors from Ireland."

2. *RIVERDANCE*

This hugely successful Irish step dance extravaganza started as a seven-minute dance act on the 1994 "Eurovision Song Contest" and has since blossomed into an internationally acclaimed touring company of more than 180 trained step dancers. The show itself integrates classic Celtic themes with step dance choreography and original music by Bill Whelan. There are three companies currently touring—the Lagan, the Lee, and the Liffey.

3. THE CLANCY BROTHERS (WITH TOMMY MAKEM)

Archetypal Irish ballad band that struck it big in the folk scene of the fifties Greenwich Village scene, these four sons of Tipperary melded an act out of straight singing in unison accompanied by guitar and tin whistle, with a relaxed manner that made later folk artists appear positively uptight.

They attracted nationwide attention when they appeared on the *Ed Sullivan Show* in 1961, and they continued to tour for the next few decades with their repertoire of standards and rebel songs of the Emerald Isle.

For the record the three original Clancy brothers were Pat, Tommy, and Liam. (The band has seen some turnover over the years.)

4. **DENNIS DAY**

Born in 1918, Day got his start on radio and was soon welcomed into Jack Benny's ensemble for his radio and, later, TV series, eventually earning his own series in 1953. Dubbed "America's Favorite Irish Tenor," Day was a frequent guest at Irish festivals and Irish-themed shows despite the fact that he was New York City born and bred.

5. *THE LORD OF THE DANCE*

Originating as a looser, more contemporary take on the themes and steps of *Riverdance*, *The Lord of the Dance* and its sequel, *Feet of Flames*, were conceived and choreographed by American-born high stepper Michael Flatley who step danced to fame as the principal male dancer in the original *Riverdance* company (Flatley is also an accomplished flautist and a champion Golden Gloves boxer).

Both *Lord of the Dance* and *Feet of Flames* are showier than *Riverdance* and come across as closer to a Vegas stage show than an Irish step dancing exhibition, which might account for their greater success on the international stage.

6. **JAMES GALWAY**

Born in 1939 in Belfast, flautist Galway played with the London Symphony Orchestra, the Royal Philharmonic, and the Berlin Philharmonic, before striking out on his own as Ireland's favorite piping soloist. His repertoire ranges from classical to folk to pop, with numerous side trips along the way with the aid of pennywhistles and fifes.

Galway is truly the Emerald Isle's king of the woodwinds as evidenced by his numerous sold-out concerts and internationally best-selling albums as well celebrity duets with numerous musical superstars.

7. DAVE ALLEN

Born in Dublin in 1936, Allen is known primarily as the host and writer of *Dave Allen at Large*, but he is also a gifted stand-up monologuist who even had a limited run on Broadway, where he mused about all things entertaining for two hours, unafraid of venturing into topical areas concerning his own Irish nationalism. At one point he made reference to some of his Irish idiosyncrasies and then used the mike stand as a minesweeper (just to be on the safe side).

8. ENYA

Born Eithne Ni Bhraonain in Gweedore, County Donegal, in 1961, Enya started her music career performing with other members of her family in the band, Clannad from 1980 to 1982 before striking out on her own as a new age Celtic soloist. She has also had a lot of success with music soundtracks, starting with the BBC TV series, *The Celts*, and such big-budget projects as *L.A. Story* and *The Lord of the Rings*.

9. THE FLEADH

Think Woodstock with pennywhistles and Guinness stout. From the Gaelic for "a gathering for music," the Fleadh (pronounced *flah*) of old tradition has been reintroduced recently with sponsors such as Guinness as a music venue of Celtic, folk, and contemporary festival whose acts range from Black 47 to Bob Dylan.

Others, such as the Town of Galway, have adopted the concept of the Fleadh for their own film festival each July, which has garnered a certain amount of critical success.

10. **THE IRISH BREAKFAST BAND**

Emblematic of the grassroots resurgence of the popularity of all things Irish in the United States, the Irish Breakfast Band was formed in the late 1990s by a diverse group from Washington, D.C., Northern Virginia, and Maryland that meets every Saturday morning for a potluck Irish breakfast and a few hours of jamming Celtic tunes.

Band leader is Sean Doherty, a retired judge who took up the fiddle as a hobby, and the eight- to twelve-musician group (their number varies from performance to performance) usually has a guest soloist on hand. The group already has a CD (*Sean's Treasure*) to its credit and has played at the John F. Kennedy Center for the Performing Arts in Washington, D.C., as well as at assorted other venues and occasions.

Engineers, Explorers, and Men of Science

Discoverers seek out new opportunities. Sometimes on the other side of the world, other times in their own backyard. Some observe and record, others design and improve, still others deduce and theorize. None of the discoverers here recognized the limits of human endurance because in their minds the limits did not exist.

1. ROBERT BOYLE

Born in Lismore, County Waterford, in 1627, of noble birth, Boyle studied at Oxford, openly questioned the prevailing beliefs and principles of alchemical studies, and advocated a more controlled procedure of experimentation and observation that provided the basis for the so-called scientific method.

In addition to his innovative use of litmus to grade acid and base, his analysis of elements, and his invention of the match, Boyle is most probably best known for Boyle's Law: At a constant temperature the volume of a gas is inversely proportional to the pressure.

Boyle's Dublin tombstone reads: "Father of Chemistry and Uncle of the Earl of Cork."

2. ERNEST HENRY SHACKLETON

Born in County Kildare in 1874, Shackleton went to sea at the age of sixteen to travel to the Far East and America. By the age of twenty-five he had already qualified to a captain a queen's ship.

Today he is best known for his Antarctic expeditions, including scaling Mount Erebus and circumnavigating the Antarctic continent. All of his expeditions proved him to be an exceptional leader of men and an extraordinary man of science. In recognition of his accomplishments he was knighted by the queen in 1909.

Also of note is the fact that his brother is considered by many contemporary historians to be the prime suspect in the theft of the Irish Crown Jewels.

3. JOHN PHILIP HOLLAND

Born in 1840, Holland is considered to be the father of the military submarine. He began his work in Ireland in the 1860s but emigrated to the United States in 1873 to continue his work. The first of his submarines, the *Fenian Ram*, was built in 1881 and backed by the Irish American Fenian movement, which hoped to use it against the British, a plan that never quite came off.

Holland's crowning achievement was *The Holland*, which was bought by the U.S. Navy in 1895 and whose design has provided the basis for most submarines since.

4. JOHN TYNDALL

Born in County Carlow in 1820, Tyndall studied natural philosophy in Germany and was named to head the

Royal Institution in 1867. Through his experiments with light, he came up with what we now call the Tyndall effect, and he was able to explain rationally why the sky appears to be blue.

5. HANS SLOANE

Born in Killyleagh, County Down, in 1660, Sloane studied medicine in London and France, served as personal physician to George II, headed the Royal College of Physicians, and is credited with introducing the scientific method to medical practice. He was also a pioneer in medical nutrition and helped to establish the practice of inoculation for smallpox.
He is also credited as with inventing the recipe for chocolate mixed with milk.

6. JAMES HOBAN

Born in County Kilkenny in 1762, Hoban immigrated to the United States in 1789, where he gained renown as an architect. In 1792 he won the competition to design the President's residence (later called the White House) and oversaw its construction, not once but twice after it had been burned down by the British in 1814. He also was one of the supervising architects on William Thornton's design of the U.S. Capitol building.

7. AGNES MARY CLERKE

Born in Skibbereen in County Cork in 1842, Clerke became infatuated with astronomy at a very early age and began work on a history of the subject at the age of fifteen. The book, *A Popular History of Astronomy During the Nineteenth Century*, was published in 1885 to widespread critical praise despite the fact that she was not considered to be a trained astronomer. She became a member of the British Astronomical Association and an honorary member of the Royal Astronomical Association in 1903, one of only four women to have been selected for membership at the time.

8. JOHN JOLY

Born in County Offaly in 1857, this son of a Church of Ireland rector was trained at Trinity College, graduating with a degree in engineering. Joly made numerous discoveries, but is known principally for his work with radiation, using it as a means to calculate the age of rocks and, later, laying the groundwork for its use to treat cancer. Joly is also credited with developing a system for color photography.

9. JOCELYN BELL-BURNELL

Born in Belfast in 1943, Bell-Burnell studied at Glasgow, then at Cambridge, where she built a radio telescope to track quasars. In addition to discovering the first pulsar in 1967, Bell-Burnell has done pioneering work in gamma ray, infrared, X-ray, and optical astronomy.

10. ARTHUR GUINNESS

Born in County Kildare in 1725, Guinness founded the family brewery in 1756 and moved it to Dublin in 1759, where he rapidly improved the brewing process through his use of the best Irish barley and drastically improving the malting techniques. The rest is history, and for that the world is extremely grateful.

Ghosts, Spectres, and Other Spooky Stuff

Paranormal incidents often don't have a basis in fiction, but rather in local lore and second hand reminiscences on a dark and stormy night. Several of these occurrences seem awfully archetypal within the canon of weird manifestations . . . but, then again, isn't that how archetypes emerge?

1. THE WHITE LIGHT OF CROM

Spectral lights are a mainstay of followers of psychic phenomena, and whether they be faeries dancing in the dusk or just unexplained meteorological manifestations, their weirdness is without question. In Crom Bay in Upper Lough Erne, strange white balls of light, roughly twice the size of soccer balls, have been sighted on numerous occasions. Though they passed approximately one foot over the surface of the bay, they nonetheless failed to cast a reflection. No explanation has ever been offered despite the many sightings reported.

2. THE PHANTOM PARISHIONER

Samuel Penrose of Cork was a returned emigrant from South America who worked as a carpenter and was a dedicated parishioner. After sharing with acquaintances certain premonitions of his own impending death, Penrose soon had two freakish, on-the-job accidents, from which he barely escaped with his life, followed by a third that left him mortally injured. Penrose died later in a Cork hospital, after his parish priest had administered the last rites.

On the day after Penrose's funeral, according to the priest, the top half of the dead man passed by him in the church, a smile on his face, as if he was hurrying along to a favored destination. The priest felt more than a bit satisfied that he might have helped his parishioner along the way . . . though the mystery of his missing lower half was never addressed.

3. THE DEATH COACH OF BALLYDUFF

In the town of Ballyduff there appears to be a confluence of spectral activity, including sounds of activity from abandoned mills and ghostly haunts that are invisible to the naked eye. Of particularly fear-inspiring note is a spectral death coach draped in black drawn by six black steeds and led by an equally black-draped coachman—both horses and master all decidedly headless. It is believed that the coach's appearance coincides with a death in the town, and that perhaps it provides transport to the next world. Similar death coaches have been spotted in counties Clare, Cork, and Limerick (as related in Croker's *Legends of Southern Ireland*).

4.   THE GHOSTLY ARCHBISHOP OF DUBLIN LIBRARY

Probably the most famous clerical ghost in all of Ireland is that of Archbishop Narcissus March, the founder of the Dublin Library. According to legend, he still prowls the shelves in search of messages left for his niece by one of his clerics with whom she eventually, much to his chagrin, eloped. Perhaps he's still trying to catch them in the act and prevent the dishonor they brought upon him.

5.   THE SPIRITUAL CONTACTS OF WILLIM BUTLER YEATS

In addition to his work as a poet and playwright, Yeats was also an aficionado of all things weird and faerie and edited such memorable volumes on the subject as *Irish Fairy and Folk Tales*. More than just being interested in the Celtic legends of the other side from the distant past, Yeats was also more than a bit involved with the contemporary spiritualism movement and took part in numerous séances. More than one source credits him with making contact with the ghost of a young man by the name of Harold Blake at Renvyle House in Connemara. The same sources also indicated that his wife, George, was an even stronger psychic than her husband.

6.   ST. PATRICK'S BELL

According to legend St. Patrick rid Ireland of snakes, reptiles, and other slimy creatures by ringing his bell at the edge of a cliff and then throwing it over into the sea, whereupon the undesirable critters followed it. The bell was then returned to the saint by angelic hands. Pilgrims making the ascent of Croagh Patrick have claimed to have heard the bell and drawn strength from it during their arduous climb. Once they reach the summit, however, there is never any evidence of the bell. As one would expect, this bell of encouragement seems to be more prevalent during the Catholic holy days of Lent and Advent.

7. THE SHELBOURNE GHOST

In 1965, a confluence of events once led to noted paranormal expert Hans Holzer (author of such classics as *Yankee Ghosts*) and psychic Sybil Leek (author of *Diary of a Witch*) being guests at Dublin's Shelbourne Hotel at the same time and witnessing/experiencing a contact from the beyond.

According to Leek she was visited by a small crying child during the night who climbed into bed with her seeking comfort. Leek felt her presence all night and in the morning her arm felt as though there had been pressure on it for several hours despite the fact that no living person had entered her locked room.

With Holzer's assistance Leek went into a trance and contacted the spirit, a young girl by the name of Mary Masters who was quite sickly and searching for her older sister, Sophie. Research indicated that the Shelbourne actually comprised several other buildings that had been on the site, and that Mary had probably died of cholera back in 1846 in one of these houses.

8. BANSHEE'S THREE

The Shane Castle Banshee (also known as the O'Neill Banshee), the O'Donnell Banshee, and the O'Brien Banshee make up this trio of tales. All three are remarkably similar and always cast the banshee as a wailing woman of great beauty (sometimes a spurned lover, sometimes a faerie revenant) whose cries make her presence known to some visitor of an ancestral home (sometimes she makes eye contact, other times she is oblivious to her observers). In all three cases these apparitions act as harbingers of a death in the family (usually a member in some other location), and, in most cases, the time of death coincides with the appearance of the banshee.

Numerous other ancestral families of Ireland lay claim to banshees, though there is no precise registry of all of them.

9. THE GHOST OF MAYNOOTH COLLEGE

A pleasant Georgian town west of Dublin, Maynooth is the home of Maynooth College, the site of a college curse story.

As the legend goes (and has been retold to countless new freshman each year) Room 2 of Rhetoric House was the sight of a student suicide by means of a razor. For the next two years the resident of that room met a similar fate until, during the third year, the similarly possessed new student opted to throw himself out the window, instead, breaking many bones, but still surviving. From that point on no new students consented to live in Room 2, so by Trustee resolution on October 23, 1860, the room was converted into an Oratory of St. Joseph, with a small altar in place of the room's back wall.

Since that decree St. Joseph has watched over new students, and no razor-wielding suicides have revisited Rhetoric House.

10. THE POLTERGEIST OF COONAN

Local rumor in Brookeborough, County Fermanagh, has it that a certain house where a murder had occurred seems to have become uninhabitable, or so it would seem due to the short duration of each new occupant. In addition to "normal" manifestations of poltergeist activity (objects being thrown around by an invisible force), there have been ghost sightings in bedrooms, disembodied snoring, and a piano that played itself. Three attempted exorcisms have yielded few or no results.

Sprites, Spirits, and Superstitions

And if spooky stuff weren't enough, when a place is as magical as the Emerald Isle, it's only natural that faerie lore blossoms in abundance. Whether tales of mythical beings, the old one, or just folk advice of an outrageous nature, the Emerald Isle has no shortage.

1. LEPRECHAUNS

Probably the most popular component of Irish lore, the leprechaun is a decidedly minor character in the pantheon of Irish mythos (more on them in the next chapter).

2. SIDHE

These faerie folk of the pre-Christian tradition are believed to be connected to the Celtic pantheons. The word, sidhe (pronounced *she*), is derived from the word that originally meant a mound of earth, thus leading to early superstitions concerning enchanted faerie mounds.

3. BEAN SI

Pronounced *banshee*, the bean si is a bodiless female spirit whose wail is thought to foretell the death of a family member. This spirit has been immortalized in numerous tales of the oral tradition as well as in stories of the fantastic by such notable authors as Ray Bradbury. It has even been incorporated into the DC Universe of comics as a nemesis of Superman.

Two Irish carvings illustrate some of the legendary "wee folk" of the country.

4. MERROW

Also known as the seafolk, the male merrow is considered to be a harbinger of good luck and is alleged to frequent the coasts in search of cases of brandy from ships that have been lost offshore. The female merrow, or the mermaid, is more attractive and seductive than her male counterpart but is usually considered a portent of bad luck, bad weather, and impending danger.

5. FETCH

From Celtic mythology, the fetch is a sort of doppelganger of mystical origin born at exactly the same moment as yourself and who allegedly wants to replace you and will do so should you ever come face to face with it.

6. POOKA

Mischievous faerie of Ireland whose persona varies from a dark stallion to a deformed goblin to a hairy bogeyman, depending on where it's seen. The sight of a pooka can stop a hen from laying eggs, sour a cow's milk, and deceive travelers on dark, lonely roads—all in all, a very destructive and mischievous faerie.

7. THE WATER HORSE

According to legend, water horses, called Nykur, were foaled in water and resemble normal horses, except that their hooves appear to be on backward. They are also shape changers who lure their riders to a river to drown them. Given the Irishman's love for his horses (as evidenced by the penal law that restricted their ownership), it was natural that an evil horse spirit would enter the pantheon, taking its place next to the enticing spectral female spirits meant to lead men astray to their doom.

8. TUATHA DE DANANN

Believed to be the earliest inhabitants of Ireland according to legend, these mystical beings retreated to a land below the earth's surface, but they occasionally surface to wreak havoc. Their name means people of the goddess, Danu.

9. THE BLARNEY STONE

Allegedly given by a witch to the king of Munster, who saved her from drowning, this stone—which is built into the battlements of Blarney Castle—is supposed to endow a visitor with the gift of blarney and a bit of luck provided he or she bends over backward to kiss it.

10. AND, OF COURSE, LOCAL SUPERSTITIONS

"If the palm of your hand itches, money is coming your way."

"The breaking of a mirror causes seven years of bad luck."

"If your ear itches and is red and hot to the touch, someone is badmouthing you behind your back."

"Red-headed women are always [insert your adjective of choice] and more so their husbands."

Many of these pass by word of mouth from one generation to the next, and new ones are added by each new generation.

Leprechauns

Without a doubt the most famous denizens of the Emerald Isle are its little people . . . its very little people if the legends are to be believed.

1. ETYMOLOGY

The word, leprechaun, is derived from either the Gaelic, "luachrma'n," which means pygmy, or "leith brogan," which means maker of one shoe.

2. REWARDS

There are several rewards for a catching a leprechaun: three wishes, a pot of gold, or the luck of the Irish, though each potential reward can be placed in jeopardy by the merest of technicalities.

3. WISHES

If a leprechaun grants you three wishes, and you wish for a fourth, you lose everything you gained from the first three. See what we mean about technicalities?

4. LUCKY CHARMS

Arthur Anderson provided the voice of Lucky the Leprechaun of Lucky Charms cereal fame.

5. FAMILY TREE

According to legend a leprechaun is of low birth amid the fey folk, his parents being an evil spirit father and a degenerate faerie mother.

6. GIDDYUP!

The favorite amusement of the leprechaun is riding sheep or goats—or even riding a dog as if it were a horse.

7. JENNIFER ANISTON

Before the co-star of the hit TV show, *Friends*, hit the big time, Jennifer Aniston made her major motion picture debut in *Leprechaun*, starring Warwick Davis.

8. DISNEY

Walt Disney used many of the same special effects in the movie, *The Gnome Mobile*, as were used in *Darby O'Gill and the Little People*, despite the fact that there are major differences in the lores of gnomes and leprechauns.

9. "THE LUSTY LEPRECHAUN"

The *Sun* has dubbed hot young actor Colin Farrell (*Jungleland* and *The Recruit*), "The Lusty Leprechaun." Why? He has admitted that he always shows up for the first day of a new shoot wearing his shamrock-emblazoned lucky boxer shorts.

10. **MADE FOR TV**

Macauley (*Home Alone*) Culkin's brother, Kieran, played a leprechaun named Barney in the NBC miniseries, *The Magical Legend of the Leprechauns.*

Sports Figures and Accomplishments

When one thinks of sports in Ireland one immediately conjures images of Gaelic games, hurling and curling, and red-headed feats of strength . . . but, needless to say, that's far from a complete picture of the sport scene on the Emerald Isle. Indeed, the Irish have made contributions at the Olympic level, as well as the professional level, in areas as diverse as Formula One racing, snooker, and, of course, boxing.

1. IRISH HOCKEY UNION

In 1892 W. E. Petersen of the High School of Dublin drew up the rules for hockey. The following year the Irish Hockey Union was formed, followed by the ladies' association the year after.

In 1908 the Irish team won the silver medal at the London Olympic Games, and although Ulster-born players participated in medal-winning teams in later Olympics, they competed under the British team flag, not Ireland's own.

2. HORSE RACING

More than a sport, horse racing is a passion for the Irish (it's no wonder that one of the penal laws was aimed directly at sadistically separating Irish owners from their best steeds). Among the numerous equestrian accolades of the Emerald Isle are:

* Red Rum, who is considered to be the most successful race horse in Irish history, having won the Grand National three times (1973, 1974, and 1977);
* Shergar, who won the 1981 Epsom Derby by the largest margin in the race's history. Shergar was later horsenapped, and the case was never really solved. It was assumed that Shergar was destroyed by her captors, but the insurance companies refused to pay her owners because there was no proof of her death by the time the policy expired; and
* Arkle, (foaled in Kilkenny), who is considered to have been the greatest steeplechaser of all time.

The Isle has also seen a an equal number of superior jockeys, such as Richard Dunwoody, born in 1964 in County Down, who has ridden more than a thousand winners in his career.

3. ALEX HIGGINS

Born in 1949 in Belfast, Alex Higgins became the youngest player (at the age of twenty-three) to take the Embassy World Snooker Championship by defeating John Spencer. His volatility earned him the nickname, "Hurricane," and in 1982 Higgins won the World Professional Snooker Championship for a second time, beating Welsh master player Ray Reardon.

4. **JOEY DUNLOP**

Born in 1952 in County Antrim, Dunlop was nick-named, "the King of the Roads," for his motorcycle prowess. In 1982 he won the Formula One motorcycle world championship. Over the next few years Dunlop won the title four more times, but he died in a race in 2000 in Estonia.

5. **SONIA O'SULLIVAN**

Born in 1969 in County Cork, O'Sullivan is an international track star of great renown. Among her accomplishments are winning the fifteen hundred meters world title at the World Student Games in 1992, the European three thousand meters title in 1994, and the gold medal in the five thousand meters at the 1995 world championships, as well as subsequent titles at the 1998 World Cross Country Championships and the European Championships, after which she took a leave from training to have a baby.

6. **MICHELLE SMITH**

Born in 1969 in County Dublin, Michelle Smith (De Bruin) made Olympic Irish history in 1996 by becoming Ireland's first female medal winner with golds in the women's four hundred individual medley, four hundred freestyle, and two hundred individual medley swimming events, as well as the bronze in the two hundred butterfly. To a certain extent some of her accomplishments have been called into question by allegations of urine sample tampering during testing, a charge she vociferously denies.

7. STEPHEN ROCHE

Born in Dublin in 1959, Roche became a world-renowned cyclist, and in 1987 was only the second cyclist to win the Tour de France, the Tour de Italy, and the world professional road race championship, all in the same year.

8. BARRY MCGUIGAN

Born in County Monaghan in 1961, boxer Barry McGuigan ("Finbar Patrick") won the Irish and Commonwealth bantam weight titles in 1978, then turned professional in 1980. He won the British featherweight title in 1983, and two years later he defeated Eusebio Pedroza of Panama for the World Boxing Association crown.

9. EDDIE IRVINE

Born in Newtownards, County Down, in 1965, Eddie began his racing career in the Formula Ford category, securing two championships between 1983 and 1987. He won his first Formula I race at the Australian Grand Prix in 1977 as part of the Ferrari team.

10. MICHAEL CARRUTH

Born in Dublin in 1967, Carruth, under his father's training, secured several local and regional titles in lightweight boxing at an early age. Between 1987 and 1990 Carruth won four senior national titles in three different weight classes, and at the 1992 Olympics he won a gold medal in the welterweight category in boxing, Ireland's first gold in the sport.

Ireland's Contributions to Rock 'n' Roll

Rock 'n' roll may be a universal language, but sometimes it is most distinctive when spoken with a brogue. More than just injecting their own cultural heritage into the music (a pennywhistle here, a jig there), several of these rock 'n' rollers have had a profound influence beyond rock 'n' roll, exerting a positive force on such issues as world hunger and freedom from oppression. One might even be tempted to say that some have formed their own IR&RA (Irish Rock 'n' Roll Army) for world peace.

1. **U2**

Formed in Dublin in 1977, U2 is without a doubt the most commercially successful rock 'n' roll band ever to come out of the Emerald Isle. Composed of Bono (born Paul Hewson), "The Edge" (born Dave Evans), Adam Clayton, and Larry Mullen, U2's brand of kick-ass rock 'n' roll is freely grown from its members' local roots ("Sunday, Bloody Sunday" dealing with the conflict in Northern Ireland), political causes (such as

Band Aid), musical inspirations from traditional American rock 'n' roll and rhythm 'n' blues, and even European techno and dance club sound. Among the group's most successful albums are *The Joshua Tree*, *The Unforgettable Fire*, and *Achtung Baby*.

Bono has achieved supercelebrity status as an international humanitarian ambassador and altruistic heir to the mantle of John Lennon.

2. VAN MORRISON

Born George Ivan Morrison, Van Morrison is a successful singer, songwriter, and saxophonist with a career spanning more than thirty-five years and including such memorable albums as *Astral Weeks*, *Veedon Fleece*, and *Avalon Sunset*, and the international hit, *Moondance*, which was featured in the movie, *An American Werewolf in London*.

At the band's "Last Waltz" concert (as well as in the movie and on the soundtrack), Morrison belted out a spirited version of the old Irish standard, "Toora Loora Loora."

3. THE CORRS

Born and raised in the Irish town of Dundalk, eleven miles south of the Ulster border, the Corrs is the latest Irish band to achieve international stardom, having already appeared with guest performances by Mick Fleetwood (of Fleetwood Mac and the Zoo), Ron Wood (of the Rolling Stones), and the father of the current Irish rock 'n' roll movement, Bono of U2 fame. Composed of three beautiful sisters (Andrea—lead vocalist and tin whistle, Caroline—vocals and percussion, and Sharon—vocals and fiddle) and their brother, Jim (vocals, guitar, and keyboards), this band's Irish fusion of the Carpenters, the Pogues, and the

Cranberries has already earned them a VH1 special (*Live in Dublin*) as well as several soundtrack appearances in addition to such top forty hits as "Breathless" and "When the Stars Go Blue."

The fact that Andrea Corr has frequently been voted the sexiest woman alive is also worthy of note.

4. SINEAD O'CONNOR

Despite having almost committed commercial career suicide by ripping up a picture of Pope John Paul II while appearing on *Saturday Night Live*, and refusing to allow "The Star Spangled Banner" to be played at the opening of a concert, Sinead O'Connor has been Ireland's angry young woman of rock 'n' roll blessed with the most unlikely voice of an angel. Her renditions of such soulful ballads as Prince's "Nothing Compares 2 U," and Rodgers and Hart's "Bewitched, Bothered and Bewildered," as well as her spirited rockin' singles like "The Emperor's New Clothes," prove that it was more than her pretty face and her bald pate that brought her such widespread popularity despite all of the controversy surrounding her.

Her most recent album, *Sean-Nos Nua*, is primarily composed of new renditions of ancient and traditional Irish melodies.

5. THE COMMITMENTS

Spawned from Alan Parker's 1991 film version of Roddy Doyle's eponymous novel about a group of working-class youths who form a band to bring soul music to Dublin, the Commitments performed their own renditions of classic Wilson Pickett, James Brown, Otis Redding, Aretha Franklin, Percy Sledge, and other legends of soul for the film's soundtrack, which immediately became an international bestseller.

Two years later several of the actor/singer/musicians from the film (including Dick Massey, Kenneth McClusky, Michael Aherne, Dave Finnegan, Robert Arkins, and Johnny Murphy) got together for a reunion tour around England. The tour was extended, and the group has continued to perform all over the world stressing the soulful affinities of the oppressed working classes, whether they be from Motown or Dublin or anywhere else on Planet Earth.

6. THE POGUES

Originally called Pogue Mahone, Gaelic for "kiss my ass," the band was formed in 1982 when Shane MacGowan (formerly of The Nipple Erectors) fell in with tin whistle player Spider Stacey and Jim Fearnley on guitar to perform their own renditions of some traditional Irish tunes. MacGowan updated their content and sound to later Irish literary renaissance with a smattering of anti-Thatcher politics, and in no time at all they were opening for the Clash.

One of the group's liner notes referred to them as "a hybrid between the Sex Pistols and the Chieftains," and the band grew in size as other joined, but rumors of drugs and alcoholism and band politics eventually drove them apart (at one point MacGowan was replaced by former Clash singer Joe Strummer, who had produced one of the Pogues' earlier albums).

7. THE CRANBERRIES

Born in the suburbs of Limerick in 1990, The Cranberries (originally called, "Cranberry Saw Us") include Dolores O'Riordan (vocals/guitar/keyboard), Fergal Lawlor (percussion), Noel Hogan (guitar, back-up vocals) and Mike Hogan (bass). The group's music is primarily a fusion of traditional Gaelic folk music with rock 'n' roll. Their debut album in 1991 was entitled, *Uncertain*, followed by *Everybody Else Is Doing It, So Why Can't We?* The band came to international prominence and exposure when it was the opening act for Duran Duran on their 1993 international tour.

8. HORSLIPS

Possibly the first rock band to combine traditional Celtic music with modern rock, Horslips was formed in 1970 and continued to infuse its music with aspects of Irish mythology in concept albums up until the group faded from the scene in 1979 (roughly coinciding with the advent of U2). Probably Horslips' most famous album was *The Book of Invasions—A Celtic Symphony*, released in 1977.

9. BOB GELDOF AND THE BOOMTOWN RATS

Originally formed in Dublin, the Rats are most prominently remembered for the truly darkly comic ode to nihilism, "(Tell me Why) I Don't Like Mondays"; however, their lead singer, Bob Geldof, eclipsed their fame with his starring role in Alan Parker's movie, *Pink Floyd: The Wall*, and his internationally role as the organizer of Live Aid to combat world hunger.

10. THIN LIZZY

Coming out of Ireland in the 1970s and led by singer and bassist Phil Lynott, Thin Lizzy had numerous international hits, including "Whiskey in the Jar," "The Boys Are Back in Town," "Jailbreak," and "Do Anything You Want To." The group disbanded in 1982 because of financial problems and Lynott's heroin habit.

Gems of Irish TV

Even though most of these series have their roots in the BBC, they are unmistakably Irish and all that entails. From sitcoms to rival the best of Norman Lear to Emerald Isle equivalents of Captain Kangaroo and Johnny Carson, the viewing of the green is evident even on black and white TVs.

1. *BALLYKISSANGEL*

A heartwarming yet contemporary comedy, *Ballykissangel* is the name of a rural Irish village where a young priest from England is sent. His new parish is full of fun eccentrics, scheming scalawags, and the usual lot of sitcom saints and sinners, but what really separates *Ballykissangel* from formula sitcoms of its ilk is its wit and relevance to day-to-day life, which is never simple enough to wrap up in a half-hour episode.

2. *ROAR*

Before achieving hunkdom in such feature films as *10 Things I Hate About You*, *The Patriot*, and *A Knight's Tale*, the Aussie thespian Heath Ledger played a Celtic prince named Conor in *Roar*, a thud-and-blunder adventure series set in Ireland around 400 CE.

3. *THE IRISH RM*

Peter Bowles of *Rumpole of the Bailey* and *To the Manor Born* fame plays Major Sinclair Yeates, who, in 1900, takes up residence in an Irish country house, having accepted the position of RM (rural magistrate—sort of local justice of the peace appointed by the crown). The series was loosely based on the book, *Some Experiments of an Irish RM*, by Edith Somerville and Martin Ross.

4. *ROS NA RUN—THE TOWN OF SECRETS* (IN IRISH)

Set against the scenic landscape of the Connemara coast, *Ros Na Run* is a contemporary Irish soap opera that fuses the day-to-day town life of Connemara Gaeltacht with cosmopolitan intrigues and concerns that spice up the lives of the townsfolk. All of the characters have secrets, some sinister, some sweet, and the cast is richly contemporary, including a gay couple and a family of transplanted Dubliners.

5. *THE MYSTIC KNIGHTS OF TIR NA NOG*

The first American television series to be filmed entirely in Ireland, *The Mystic Knights of Tir Na Nog* (which supposedly means "land of youth") is a Celtic equivalent of *The Power Rangers*—no more, no less.

6. *MUINTIR NA DARACH—PEOPLE OF THE OAK* (IN IRISH)

This show focuses on the high jinks and tribulations of three friends who inadvertently release the spirits of three monks from a cursed oak tree that trapped them when they tried to salvage relics of St. Malachy's tabernacle over a thousand years ago.

7. *FATHER TED*

Described by one British newspaper as "a winning combination of tittering nuns, drunken priests and a housekeeper from hell," *Father Ted* is the anti-*Ballykissangel*, featuring overly broadly drawn characters of the *Fawlty Towers* variety. Three wayward Catholic priests are exiled/assigned to a parish in the northern islands of Ireland after having committed acts of great embarrassment, ineptitude, and/or scandal . . . and events of a definitely less-than-serious nature ensue.

8. *C U BURN*

Way before HBO's *Six Feet Under* was this story of a pair of quirky brothers who are undertakers in Donegal and set up the first turf-burning crematorium. It is blackly comic and more than a little politically incorrect.

9. *DAVE ALLEN AT LARGE*

This show is sort of Dean Martin à la the BBC, except that Allen, though he always has a drink in one hand and a cigarette in the other, never appears to be drunk and, indeed, typifies the sophisticated barfly of the swinging singles seventies. Allen was always equally comfortable with humor about the politics, sex, and religion of the post-Playboy generation, and his witty monologues were supported by the requisite number of guest spots, skits, and variety numbers.

10. *Wanderly Wagon*

Considered by many to be the classic Irish children's TV program, *Wanderly Wagon* was sort of *Captain Kangaroo* meets *Dr. Who* and featured a human cast of players supplemented by puppets that included Judge (a dog who was the brains of the outfit), Mr. Crow (a wry crow passing himself off as the wagon's cuckoo clock), and Sneaky Snake (who was just as his name described). The cast traveled in a flying wagon that was able to take them to outer space or to any place in Ireland.

The Emerald Isle in Emmy Contention

Not everyone of Irish descent on American television is a cop, though sometimes it seems that way. From Manhattan bars to western saloons, from brogue-spouting priests to dulcet-toned demons, from the blue bloods of Boston to the barflies of the Bowery, descendants of the Emerald Isle appear on all of the major networks.

1. *RYAN'S HOPE*

This long-running (1975–1989) soap opera derived its name from the eponymous Irish pub owned by the Ryans (Johnny and Maeve, as played by Bernard Barrow and Helen Gallagher), whose three generations of family members and their Upper West Side New York exploits, involvements, and scandals made this an afternoon favorite of numerous housewives, Irish and otherwise.

2. **THE LASSITER FAMILY on** *BEACON HILL*

Think of this as *Dallas* done Irish-American in 1920s
Boston with the robber baron Lassiter family, with the
family patriarch played by Stephen Elliott, replacing
the Ewings of Dallas. Originally billed as an American
version of the BBC hit, *Upstairs, Downstairs*, with the
downstairs staff also mostly composed of Irish émi-
grés, the drama never progressed beyond primetime
soap status without the significant class commentary
that was so much a part of the BBC series' success.

3. **KATHY WILLIAMS on** *THE DANNY THOMAS SHOW/MAKE
    ROOM FOR DADDY*

Marjorie Lord played Kathy, nicknamed Clancey, the
second wife of Lebanese-American singer Danny
Williams, who played the part as a fiery redhead. She
was outspoken and always ready to get her Irish up
during arguments with her hot-tempered husband
about family, friends, and business that, despite the
shouting, were always resolved with a kiss and hug by
the episode's end.

4. **DOYLE on** *ANGEL*

Dublin-born Glenn Quinn assayed the role of a
demidemon (half-human, half-demon) during the first
season of this spin-off from the successful *Buffy the
Vampire Slayer* series. Doyle was cursed with precog-
nitive visions that hit him like a sledgehammer against
the cranium and provided a clue to the next good deed
that had to be performed by Angel, the vampire with a
soul, played by the devilishly good-looking David
Boreanaz.

Viewers who only knew Quinn from his punkish stint on the reprehensible *Roseanne* show never realized that his accent on *Angel* was the real thing; midwestern Mark the dullard was the put-on.

5.   SERGEANT MORGAN O'ROURKE on *F TROOP*

This Irish conman cavalry sergeant played by Forrest Tucker made no secret of his Emerald Isle roots, including memorable episodes where his father (also played by Tucker) visited from Ireland or the occasional Irish tune sung in the saloon, such as "Donegal."

Forrest Tucker had made a name for himself in such films as *The Crawling Eye* and *Auntie Mame*, but he will probably be remembered in Hollywood circles as Arthur Godfrey's well-hung sidekick.

6.   CHESTER A. RILEY in *THE LIFE OF RILEY*

As played by Jackie Gleason and, later, William Bendix, this Los Angeles–based sitcom of the *Father Knows Best* era was played primarily for laughs, with blue-collar Chester A. Riley always scheming to get ahead or just cope with modern life, a model for future characters such as Ralph Cramden and perhaps even Homer Simpson.

7.   FATHERS O'MALLEY AND FITZGIBBON in *GOING MY WAY*

Gene Kelly and Leo G. Carroll played the roles made famous by Bing Crosby and Barry Fitzgerald in the film of the same name, curate and pastor of a poor New York parish. Though their portrayals were less Irish than those in the film, they were nonetheless the stereotypic Irish priests.

8. *THE Cavanaughs*

Christine Ebersole played Kit Cavanaugh, showgirl black sheep of the Cavanaugh clan who returns to South Boston to live with her crusty old father (Barnard Hughes with the requisite brogue). Other family members include a widowed brother and his very Catholic kids, her Jesuit brother, and her even more of a black sheep Uncle James (played by Art Carney).

9. WILLIAM MICHAEL FRANCIS ALOYSIUS "BUB" O'CASEY on *MY THREE SONS*

Steve Douglas's father-in-law as played by William Frawley moved in with the widower and his three sons after his daughter's death, a curmudgeonly cook/maid/nanny to the brood. When Frawley died (and was replaced by "Uncle Charlie" as played by William Demarest), his character was written off the series by having him win the Irish Sweepstakes, thus allowing him to go on a vacation to Farnsea, Ireland, where he had family . . . and whence he never returned.

10. GEORGE O'GRADY on *THE GEORGE CARLIN SHOW*

Think of Carlin's persona as next-generation Irish curmudgeon, as his George O'Grady is a past middle age, pony-tailed cab driver who still leads a blue-collar bachelor existence that includes hanging out at Moylan's Tavern with other ne'er-do-wells.

Irish-American Politicians Past and Present

America is built on a foundation of many different cultures and ethnic groups, but no single one has done a better job of influencing the country's political system than Irish Americans. Men (and women) of the people with a real appreciation for working-class issues have provided platforms for many politicos whose ancestors have heralded from the Emerald Isle.

All of them tough and headstrong, even those who in the long run wound up being more masters of blarney than custodians of the public good.

1. ANDREW JACKSON

Born to Scotch-Irish parents in 1767, Jackson, also known as "Old Hickory," was the seventh president of the United States. He was finally elected after having won the popular vote in the election four years earlier, but losing to John Quincy Adams when the confusing four-man race wound up being decided in the House of Representatives.

A self-made man and war hero, Jackson is also considered to be the founder of the Democratic Party.

2. JOHN F. KENNEDY

It took more than a hundred years for another Irish American to win the White House, but in 1960, John F. Kennedy became the second Irish-American Democrat to win the White House as well as the first Catholic and the youngest person ever elected to the office.

Born to a self-made, financially successful Irish-American family of robber baron origins, Kennedy became the epitome of a working-class/blue blood mythos that has remained with the family to this day, despite its many scandals and hardships, as it continues to fight for civil rights.

3. ALFRED E. SMITH

Irish American on his mother's side, German Italian on his father's, Al Smith was a melting pot American who rose from a boyhood job at the Fulton Fish Market to the New York governor's mansion. He was also an unsuccessful presidential candidate on the Democratic ticket in 1928, the first Catholic to run for the office on a major party ticket.

4. RICHARD CROKER

Irish–born, New York Democratic politician and boss of Tammany Hall, Croker established a monopoly on civic services and public affairs in the 1890s through a system of widespread graft, corruption, and extortion in the tradition of his predecessors, Boss Tweed and "Honest John" Kelly.

He was ousted from office in 1901, and immigrated back to Ireland with a trunk load of money. He purchased a substantial estate and lived out his days as a successful horse breeder.

5. JAMES "JIMMY" WALKER

A native New Yorker of Irish descent, James J. Walker was the fun-loving mayor of New York during the Roaring Twenties who is credited with bringing legalized boxing to New York, via the Walker Law, that provided a model for regulation by state athletic commissions. Too much of a good time is bad for anyone, let alone a mayor, and in 1932, Walker was called to Albany by then-Governor Franklin Delano Roosevelt (who was on a law-and-order kick on his way to running for the presidency) to explain certain improprieties and matters of corruption associated with the city administration. Walker resigned shortly thereafter.

6. EDWARD "TED" KENNEDY

Youngest and sole surviving brother of John F. Kennedy, Edward Kennedy was selected to fill the U.S. Senate seat vacated by his brother in 1960 (upon his election as president) and has been reelected ever since. A champion of social causes and the "good" that government should do, Kennedy is the liberal lion of the Senate and a revered elder Democratic statesman despite the occasional overpublicized scandals that have plagued the Kennedy family name.

7. RICHARD J. DALEY

Grandson of Irish immigrants and raised on Chicago's Irish Catholic Bridgeport neighborhood in south Chicago in the early years of the twentieth century,

Daly worked his way up from the Chicago Stockyards to the office of the mayor of Chicago (a post he held for twenty-two years), where he emerged as the head of one of the country's most efficient political machines. He is also considered to be the last of the big city bosses.

8. PETER T. KING

Congressman Peter T. King is a Republican of Irish descent (and proud of it!) representing Long Island in the U.S. House of Representatives. He is known for his independence and was one a very small number of Republicans who voted against President Bill Clinton's impeachment.

King also has a second career as a novelist, with three Irish issue thrillers to his credit so far. The second of these, *Deliver Us from Evil*, includes flashbacks to the Irish peace accords and features memorable plot-related cameos by Gerry Adams, Tony Blair, and Bill Clinton.

9. SUSAN COLLINS

Daughter of an Irish-American, fifth-generation, lumbering family (the business is currently operated by her two brothers), this two-term Republican U.S. senator from Maine serves as chairman of the Government Affairs Committee charged with oversight of the Department of Homeland Security. She is only the fifteenth woman in history to be elected to the Senate.

10. EAMON DE VALERA

This esteemed prime minster of Ireland and president of the Republic was actually born in New York, the son of a Spanish father and an Irish mother. Indeed, it was probably his American citizenship (by birth) that saved him from execution and penal exile for his role in the Easter Rising of 1916 as was the fate of most of his fellow arrested conspirators.

Ireland has exported many great political minds to America, but that debt has been more than repaid by the export of de Valera to the Emerald Isle.

St. Patrick's Day Parades

This staple celebration of all things Irish was really nurtured in America rather than on the Emerald Isle. What started as a religious observance became a yearly dinner feast (with more than a bit of cause-related fund-raising) and eventually morphed into a very public celebration of the virtues of the Emerald Isle. After the parades had taken to the streets in all four corners of the world, it was only natural that such celebrations would return to Ireland and become a staple of pride there as well.

1. NEW YORK CITY

The granddaddy of this celebration of the wearing of the green dates back to post-Revolutionary War days.

2. BOSTON

The festivities in Boston followed those in New York New York as the Massachusetts city's immigrants began celebrating their all-things-Irish heritage with a thoroughly organized and sponsored affair by 1841.

3. CHICAGO

The year 1843 saw this city embrace an organized street parade in honor of the saint. Of particular note, this parade has been captured on the silver screen numerous times, such as in the 1993 film *The Fugitive*.

4. MELBOURNE, AUSTRALIA

Exiles from the Emerald Isle joined in celebrating the occasion in 1843, the same year Chicago did.

5. TORONTO, CANADA

Parade celebrations of the Emerald Isle started to occur just before the 1850s with a surprising deemphasis on the religious issues that divided the Protestants from the Catholics, in name of Canadian-Irish harmony.

6. DUBLIN

Festivals and street fairs morphed into parades sometime around 1905 but were cancelled on occasion as disagreements with the crown increased.

7. LIMERICK

The city of Limerick revived its St. Patrick's Day parades in 1962 as a demonstration of Catholic solidarity.

8. BELFAST

Participants took to the streets in 1974 in answer to the Orangeman marches, which led to numerous clashes here (and in Derry) during the Troubles.

9. WOODSIDE/SUNNYSIDE, QUEENS, NEW YORK

This parade came to prominence as an alternative to New York City's event when the Ancient Order of Hibernians began to play politics and ban the inclusion of gay groups in the festivities. Local politicians, mindful of their gay constituencies, sometimes supported this smaller, yet more inclusive, neighborhood parade.

10. AND MANY MORE . . .

Other parades were established in Holyoke and Lawrence, Massachusetts, and Rockaway Beach in Queens, which—in its inaugural year—billed itself as the world's longest St. Patrick's Day procession. For this one day, it's said that whoever celebrates the wearing of the green does honor to the Emerald Isle.

Battles on the Old Sod

Since the Emerald Isle's earliest years, the Irish have always fought to protect their land from interlopers, whether they are bellicose warlords, invading barbarians, or acquisitive agents of the crown. Irish warriors have been ready to fight at home and abroad, even when a momentary victory does not assure individual survival . . . because in many cases it hasn't.

1. THE BATTLE OF BELACH MUGNA (908)

Also called the battle of Ballaghmoon, this conflict is notable for the death of chieftain Cormac Mac Cuilennain, king and bishop of Cashel. The battle involved a dispute concerning monastic jurisdiction and the established hegemony.

2. THE BATTLE OF ISLANDBRIDGE (919)

The Battle of Islandbridge is most notable for the death of Niall Glundubh, the Black-kneed King of Tara, who died leading his men to expel the invading Vikings. He was the first High King to die at Viking hands.

3. THE BATTLE OF CLONTARF (1014)

This battle resulted in a decisive victory against the Vikings by the forces of Irish High King Brian Boru, and, of course, Boru died victorious there.

4. THE BATTLE OF GLENMALURE (1580)

Glenmalure was the site of the first defeat of Protestant Lord Grey de Wilton, who had been dispatched by the Crown to settle the numerous rebellions in the lands of the Desmonds and Munster. Undaunted by this defeat (and still alive, a rarity in itself) de Wilton led his men on to victory at Wicklow.

5. THE BATTLE OF THE YELLOW FORD (1598)

Hugh O'Neill defeated Sir Henry Bagenal's forces of the Crown in County Tyrone, the greatest Irish defeat of English forces ever, and spread the rebellion farther on to Munster, causing the Crown no lack of new headaches.

6. THE BATTLE OF RATHMINES (1649)

Colonel Jones, the Crown's Parliamentary commander in Dublin, defeated the rebel forces of Ormond that had been laying siege to the city. This battle was fought a little more than a week before Oliver Cromwell's arrival, so it was a major plus for indigenous Crown forces, who resented the coming of the new and savage Lord Protector.

7. THE SIEGE OF DERRY (1688–89)

Derry's siege, initiated when thirteen Derry apprentices loyal to William of Orange locked the city gates against the oncoming Jacobites, lasted fifteen weeks.

Though combat deaths were kept to a minimum, many of the inhabitants of the city died of starvation and disease because of the blockade.

8.   THE BATTLE OF THE BOYNE (1690)

The most commemorated incursion in Irish history, the Battle of the Boyne was fought on July 1, 1690, between the Jacobite and Williamite forces. It became a symbol of the Protestant cause in the 1790s.

9.   THE BATTLE OF AUGHRIM (1691)

A year after the Battle of the Boyne, the Jacobites were routed in Aughrim with losses so severe that their surrender at Limerick was inevitable.

10.   THE EASTER RISING (1916)

Setting the stage for the conflicts to come, this seizure of a post office and civic center ushered in the twentieth-century Troubles, as the forces for a free Ireland fought against their Crown oppressors.

Indignities and Crimes

The resiliency of the Irish people has been tested many times over the years as they strived to achieve their independence. Not all of the indignities they suffered were at the instigation of the Crown . . . just most of them.

1. PENAL LAWS

Strictly speaking, the Penal Laws refer to the set of discriminatory regulations passed in the 1690s against Roman Catholic clergy and laity. Though most of these rules ended with passage of the Catholic Relief Act in 1829, it was commonly groused concerning their elimination "that no one bothered to tell the landlords and the constables." (The next chapter includes the worst of these penal laws.)

2. POYNING'S LAW

A statute introduced by Lord Deputy Edward Poyning in 1494 mandated that all bills, laws, and amendments introduced in the Irish Parliament had to be approved first by the English Privy Council, basically undercutting the viability of all local Irish legislative authority.

3. RAMPAGE OF OLIVER CROMWELL

Though he actually spent only ten months on Irish soil (August 1649—May 1650), Cromwell and his despotic reign of terror backed by a sadistic military force effectively broke the back of the Irish resistance at the time. Once he returned to England (and emerged as Lord Protector), he passed additional anti-Irish legislation, but its enforcers were far less bloodthirsty than Cromwell ever was.

4. POTATO FAMINE

Caused by an airborne spore–based fungus, known as the potato blight, which spread throughout Ireland in 1845, causing the vast majority of the potato crop to rot in the ground, the Potato Famine (also called the Great Famine) lasted from the mid-1840s to early 1850s, resulting in the death by hunger and/or malnutrition of many in Ireland while the sovereign across the channel raised nary a finger to assist.

5. THE MARCH OF THE ORANGEMEN

The Orange Order was formed in County Armagh in 1795 as a revival of the old Orange Institution, which supported William of Orange in his victory over the Catholic James II. Over the years it evolved into a powerful and arrogant opposition force to Catholics' efforts to achieve emancipation, not dissimilar to the Ku Klux Klan in the American South.

The Orange Order exists to this day and is closely tied to the Ulster Unionists, whose annual marches through the lands over which they once claimed dominion are often the cause of added tension and violence in Northern Ireland.

6. THE BLACK AND TANS

"The Black and Tans" is the nickname of the special auxiliary force of the Royal Irish Constabulary, formed in 1920 to combat the resistance of the Irish Republican Army forces during the Anglo-Irish War. Their name is derived from the colors of their improvised black and khaki uniforms.

Though they were alleged to have comprised solely ex-soldiers, their force and ranks were supplemented by killers and felons from English prisons and other sadistic undesirables whom the Crown saw fit to export. Their prime objective was punishment rather than patrol and policing.

7. THE THEFT OF THE IRISH CROWN JEWELS

In July 1907 the Irish crown jewels were discovered missing from the safe in which they were kept in Dublin Castle. Investigation of the theft reportedly was hindered by the discovery of links between a member of the staff of Sir Arthur Vicar, Ulster king of arms, and a London-based network of socially prominent homosexuals whose connections may have extended to Edward VII's court. It is widely believed that this was directly related to an organized effort to remove so-called nationalistic artifacts from Ireland. The jewels have never been recovered, nor have the thieves ever been identified (though the brother of renowned explorer Ernest Henry Shackleton remains a prime suspect, according to most historians of the case).

8. THE MAGDALENE HOUSES

These were homes for "wayward women" set up by an alliance of the Catholic Church and the Irish state that denied women their fundamental rights as citizens and shapers of their own destiny. Though masquerading as enforced convent schools, they were little more than workhouse for those judged to be immoral and detrimental to society (and themselves).

9. BOYCOTT

This is the actual incident from which the word, boycott, was coined. Ex-overseer and agent of the Crown for County Mayo, Ireland, Charles Cunningham Boycott opposed his peasants' demands for land reform (as backed by the Irish Land League), resulting in the walking out of all of his landed workers in 1880 (their boycott). Rather than give in, Boycott hired fifty Orangemen to take in the harvest, backed by a thousand troops at a cost to the Crown of ten thousand pounds so that the tyrannical landowner would not be forced to negotiate in good faith with his landed workforce.

10. THE OPPRESSION OF CENSORSHIP

After years of oppression by the Crown, when independence and Catholic religious freedom were attained, it was quite ironic that the new regime and powers-that-be in both church and state resulted in censorship of the exact art forms bred of the creative spirits fostered by the years of oppression.

Numerous works of art and literature, including the masterworks of O'Casey and Joyce, had to seek foreign venues for publication and presentation due to the strict censorship laws. Similarly, the film industry was hampered initially by these restrictions as well.

Relics of these laws and oppressive measures are present even today—for example, the anti-birth control/abortion legislation that still exists on the Emerald Isle.

The Worst of the Penal Laws

The Penal Laws were first written into law in 1695 expressly to penalize Catholics for their religion in a manner that not only would punish them at that time, but in essence would indenture them into powerlessness for generations to come unless they converted to Protestantism.

The laws' immediate effect was clearly to put native Roman Catholics under the thumb of the more recently arrived British immigrants and, over a short period, annex anything worth owning into the hands of the more loyal subjects of the Crown.

1. GUN OWNERSHIP

The first law, "The Act for the Better Securing of the Government against Papists," forbade Catholics from owning or bearing any "gun, pistol, or sword, or any other weapon of offense or defense, under penalty of fine, imprisonment, pillory or public whipping." It also allowed unrestricted searches of Catholic property as part of its enforcement.

2. FAREWELL, FATHER

The second law enacted, "The Bishop's Banishment Act," required all Popish clergy to leave Ireland by May 1, 1698, under penalty of transportation (indentured servitude) for life. It stated that any who returned would be hanged, drawn, and quartered.

The following laws had less grandiose titles.

3. NO RELIGIOUS FREEDOM

Another law forbade Catholics from exercising their religion or from receiving a Catholic education. Moreover, Catholics were even fined for not attending Protestant services.

4. RESTRICTED VOTING

Voting privileges were "restricted" or, put more simply, Catholics lost their right to vote.

5. NO SCHOOLING

This inclusion forbade the Catholics from sending their children abroad for an education, thus guaranteeing them a legacy of further oppression and disadvantage.

6. WORKING RESTRICTIONS

The law regarding working restrictions forbade Catholics from entering a profession, holding public office, or even engaging in trade or commerce.

7. LANDOWNING RESTRICTIONS

Another law forbade Catholics from renting any land that was worth more than thirty shillings, and, when this was deemed to be not restrictive enough, a more specific law was passed that forbade Catholics from gaining any profit from their land over a third of the land's value.

8. HORSE-OWNING RESTRICTIONS

Catholics were forbidden to own a horse worth more than five pounds, a law that was easily exploited by unscrupulous Protestants who used it as an excuse to appropriate the best new foals from their Catholic owners.

9. TOWN RESTRICTIONS

Catholics were also prohibited from living in a corporate town or within five miles of one, thus further restricting their chances of employment or a decent quality of life.

10. MORE LAND RESTRICTIONS

Under "The Act to Prevent the Further Growth of Property," Catholics were forbidden to exercise controlled preference in the division of legacies and estates, which meant that all inheritances were divided equally among all acceptable heirs.

Irish Jailbirds

Doing time was just another component of all too many Irishmen's lives, and though charges may have been mentioned or alluded to, in many cases legal due process and a fair and impartial court were sadly missing as a prerequisite to one's stay at Long Kesh or some such other facility.

For some, this prison was a stopover on the way to freedom for the Irish people. For others it was a matter of conscience or just another cog in the creative process. And for still others it was just the place they deserved to be, because even among the Irish there are occasionally criminals.

1. EAMON DE VALERA

It was perhaps only his American citizenship (he was born in Brooklyn in 1882) that saved this future president and prime minister of the Irish Free State/ Republic of Ireland from execution as one of the leaders of the rebellion known as the Easter Rising of

1916. Indeed, he was sentenced to death initially with several others but was singled out due to his American citizenship. As a result his sentence was commuted to life imprisonment, and a year later he was granted amnesty and released.

Needless to say, his early political career was littered with stays in jail on both earned and trumped up charges.

2. OSCAR WILDE

The famous wit, writer, and trendsetter of London society found himself on the wrong side of the law when a battle of wits and defamation concerning reputations and affairs of the heart (with a young lover from high society who happened to be of the same sex as Wilde) led to a lawsuit.

Wilde charged the father of his lover, Lord Alfred Douglas, with defamation over the allegation that Wilde was a sodomite (a charge that was accurate and not a secret among Wilde's circle). Wilde's ego got in the way, so sure was he that he would prevail in court on the basis of wits alone.

He was wrong. He lost the case and was immediately charged with and convicted of having performed homosexual acts and sent to prison, where he stayed from 1895 to 1897. Upon his release, bankrupt and disgraced, Wilde left Britain and went to France, where he wrote such prison-inspired works as "Ballad of Reading Gaol" and *De Profundis* (*From the Depths*) about his experience. The biographical play, *An Evening with Panthers*, is based on his mental state while he was incarcerated.

3. **GERRY ADAMS**

Adams, like his predecessor, de Valera, was no stranger to civil disobedience and the unjust incarceration that was just one of the risks of practicing it. As an early Irish Republican Army (and, later, Sinn Fein) activist, Adams was arrested and incarcerated without trial for alleged illegal activities and was held on the *Maidstone*, a British prison ship off the Irish coast. He was freed later to take part in the peace talks on behalf of the IRA, but after the talks broke down due to British lack of good faith, he was rearrested and sent away for another four years, this time at Long Kesh. His book, *Cage Eleven*, is based on his prison experiences.

4. **NED KELLY**

The son of Irish transportees in mid- to late nineteenth-century Victoria, Australia, Kelly was the eldest of eight children and became the man of the family at the age of twelve when his ex-con father died. Continuing the family tradition, Kelly was sixteen at the time of his first arrest, when he was convicted of receiving a stolen horse and sentenced to three years in prison.

Since Australian justice toward the Irish mirrored that being practiced in the rest of the British empire, Kelly's actual criminality is subject to debate; however, on his release he once again wound up on the wrong of the law, resulting in the imprisonment of his mother and a price of one hundred pounds sterling on his head.

Soon thereafter the Kelly gang was formed and became quite successful at robbing banks, earning Kelly himself a Robin Hood–like legacy, with an added aura of mystery complemented by the suit of armor adorned with a green sash that he wore in pursuit of his trade.

He was cornered and shot more than twenty-eight times in June 1880, and—following traditional due process—his wounds were tended to by the authorities who hanged him in November of 1880 at the tender age of twenty five, as a cop killer and outlaw despite the public outcry for amnesty.

5. **MARTIN CAHILL**

Known as "The General" because of his mastery of strategy and planning, Cahill started his career humbly with a conviction for burglary at the age of sixteen, for which he received two years in reform school. He followed this with a conviction for theft and possession of stolen goods at the age of twenty, and received a prison sentence of four years. Such penal setbacks have to be looked on as just youthful indiscretions and the result of immaturity and inexperience along Cahill's career path toward becoming a master criminal of the Irish underworld. Indeed, these two sentences represented the longest period he ever spent behind bars despite numerous charges against him, ranging from armed robbery and the theft of artwork worth more than thirty million pounds sterling, to political corruption and extortion.

A man of principle, Cahill avoided the narcotics trade and personally shunned such vices as smoking, drinking, and gambling, though he occasionally gave into vanity and arrogance by taunting the authorities in public with dares to arrest him. He was assassinated at the age of forty-five by a freelance IRA gunman in Dublin in 1994, and since then has been the subject of several movies, most famously John Boorman's *The General*.

6. GERRY CONLON

As the story goes there were numerous charges (mostly of a delinquency nature, perhaps as serious as drug possession and breaking and entering) that could have been leveled at Gerry Conlon. That said, he (along with his father and two others) was convicted of terrorist bombings in legislative and police procedural gymnastics and machinations that foreshadowed Attorney General John Ashcroft's inept misuse of the Patriot Act in the United States after September 11, 2001.

Conlon and the others were cleared of all charges, and three former police officers were subsequently accused of conspiring to pervert the course of justice. Three of the four were released after serving fourteen years (Conlon's father's sentence was shorter as he had earlier died in prison).

7. BRENDAN BEHAN

This Dublin-born playwright and literate man about town was educated by Christian brothers until the age of fourteen, and then by the British, beginning at age sixteen when he was arrested for his alleged involvement with the IRA. This provided fertile soil for his autobiographical classic, *Borstal Boy*, published in 1958 ("Borstal" is a "boy's prison" along the lines of a reformed school).

On his release he immediately renewed his acquaintance with matters pertaining to the IRA and was arrested again, this time for shooting at a policeman. He was sentenced to fourteen years but wound up serving only four.

His play, *The Quare Fellow*, written roughly at the same time as *Borstal Boy*, also deals with his prison experiences, and is set in the gaol (jail) on the eve of a hanging.

8. BOBBY SANDS

This patriot and martyr of the Irish cause joined the IRA while still in his teens, and though he never moved up in the actual street organization, he nonetheless evolved into a leader while incarcerated (for possession of a revolver and other disputed charges for which he was sentenced for fourteen years) as the leader of the 1981 H Block Hunger Strike in Long Kesh prison.

Among the demands of the strikers were that as "political prisoners," rather than common criminals, they deserved the right to not wear prison uniforms or be assigned prison work, to associate freely among themselves, and to organize their own activities and educational resources within the system of their confinement. They also demanded to be allowed a visit, a letter, and a parcel each week.

The strike gained international attention, and Sands was elected to the House of Commons . . . but, unfortunately, the strike failed in the long run, with Sands its first victim. He died on the sixty-sixth day in May 1981 at the age of twenty-seven.

9. DANIEL BERRIGAN

Proving that resistance and politically motivated incarcerations are not confined to lands under the aegis of the Crown, this second-generation Irish Catholic born into a working-class family in Virginia, Minnesota, and Jesuit priest was constantly at odds with the U.S. government during the President Richard Nixon's administration. Berrigan engaged in numerous nonviolent protests (including destroying draft records in

Catonsville, Maryland, along with eight other activists, who came to be known as "The Catonsville Nine").

When a warrant was issued for his arrest, he quietly went underground for awhile, until he was finally apprehended and sent to prison for two years.

After Nixon left the White House, Father Berrigan continued his active confrontational pacifist actions against the makers of weapons of war that have resulted in several other arrests. With each time served, he writes another book related to his confinement, a long-standing Irish tradition.

10. JAMES J. "WHITEY" BULGER

This Irish-American denizen of the FBI's Ten Most Wanted List, and a leading light of the Boston Irish mob with numerous political ties, has been charged with such crimes as racketeering, murder, extortion, narcotics, and money laundering. Bulger is currently on the lam.

Guerrilla Warriors of the Old Sod

The ongoing war in Ireland has existed for hundreds of years, with the Irish people bearing the bludgeoning of an occupational force that on numerous occasions has declared victory . . . but has never been able to bring about a peace until the close of the twentieth century. As a result, the home army of Ireland has been a grassroots movement, practicing the strategies of the underdog with all the tenacity of a hawk protecting its nest.

The great guerrilla warriors of Irish history have proven many times over that you don't need a fancy uniform or ceremonial flags and drills to be a soldier and, in the following ten cases, a damn good one at that.

1. ART OG MACMORROUGH KAVANAUGH

A fourteenth-century Irish warlord, Kavanaugh realized that although he stood no chance of breaching the Norman fortresses, he nonetheless could harass the invading forces with skirmishes and traveling strikes. Richard II of England tried twice to subdue him with the Crown's standing army but did not succeed in doing so.

2. FIACH MACHUGH O'BYRNE (C. 1544-1597)

Leader of the Gaelic resistance to Elizabethan penetration in County Wicklow, O'Byrne's ascent to power is attributed primarily to his defeat of the English forces at Glenmalure in 1580.

On-again-off-again periods of peace and resistance eventually forced him into an alliance with the Ulster Lords against the Crown toward the end of the sixteenth century in warfare that continued until his capture and execution in May 1597.

3. SHANE O'NEILL (1530-1567)

Ulster dynastic lord, O'Neill fought a guerilla campaign against his father and brothers for his right to succession with the aid of financed Scottish mercenaries. He negotiated the battlegrounds carefully, picking and choosing his targets and never engaging in conflicts where conditions did not favor his side, even arming the peasantry as an extra line of defense. Eventually Ulster politics forced him to declare war on the Scots as well while he was personally settling old scores with rivals' clans, which resulted in his surprise assassination during political negotiations.

4. HUGH O'NEILL (1550-1616)

Ulster chieftain and rebel (as well as avowed rival to the throne of Shane O'Neill), this O'Neill attempted to exert his authority over the Ulster lords while simultaneously supporting English reform policy. Eventually he and his forces were had to join in rebellion against the government in 1594.   His success at the Battle of the Yellow Ford in 1598 allowed him to carry the rebellion farther into Ireland, but he eventually wound up overextending his guerilla forces.

5.   OWEN ROE O'NEILL (C. 1590–1649)

Owen, Hugh's nephew, led an army of the Confederation of Kilkenny to defeat the English at Benburb in 1646, with a force of five thousand poorly armed men against the Crown's standing army of six thousand. To succeed he used fast-moving cavalry to split the force off from its reinforcements, sweeping back to take out the artillery, and only then laying waste to the now unsupported foot soldiers in a maneuver of which the Mongol hordes of Asia might have been proud.

6.   MICHAEL DWYER (1771-1826)

After the defeat at the Battle of Vinegar Hill, Dwyer, rebel survivor of the unsuccessful rebellion of 1798, took a surviving force of approximately ten men into the Wicklow mountains, where they maintained an active guerilla resistance that was never defeated by the British and whose ranks eventually swelled to more than 150.

7.   JAMES FINTAN LALOR (1807-1849)

Born in County Laois, Lalor was primarily a politician, journalist, and pamphleteer who worked to repeal the Act of Union (1801). He is credited with the following military maxim:

The force of England is entrenched and fortified. You must draw it out of position; break up its mass; break its trained line of march and manoueuvre, its equal step and serried array . . . nullify its tactic and strategy, as well as its discipline; decompose the science and system of war, and resolve them into their first elements [from the *Handbook for Volunteers of the Irish Republican Army*].

8. CAPTAIN MACKEY LOMASNEY

Born in Cork, Lomasney learned his guerilla craft in America while serving as a Union officer in the American Civil War. Known as "The Little Captain," Lomasney—as part of the Fenians—bedeviled numerous British garrisons on his return to Cork after his American service.

9. MICHAEL COLLINS (1890-1922)

During his tenure as leader of the Irish Volunteers (later the Irish Republican Army/IRA), Collins—the "big fella" himself—showed great skill, a keen grasp of guerilla tactics and strategy, and dedication in his mission to infiltrate the British intelligence/counterintelligence apparatus in Ireland and disrupt it, and in his successful targeting of key operatives for assassination.

10. JIM LYNAGH (1956–1987)

Commander of the East Tyrone Brigade (whose exploits of heroism date back to the days of the resistance against the Tudors in the seventeenth century), Lynagh, with Padraig McKearney, attempted to resurrect the strategy of "the flying column"—an independent, self-sustaining detachment that is mobile and immune to infiltration—that had worked so successfully against the British forces in Cork during the 1919–21 uprising.

Rebellions, Mutinies, and Rescues

One man's rebellion is another man's revolution, and the ongoing war for Irish independence dates back many centuries, with numerous skirmishes, mutinies, general strikes, and all-out riots as the will of the Irish people and the resilience of the human spirit gave evidence again and again that it would not submit to oppression at the hands of a foreign and unjust power.

1. THE EASTER RISING

At midday on Easter Sunday 1916, the Irish Volunteers and other nationalists seized the Dublin General Post Office and other civic buildings in the area, inciting riots and rebellions all around the city. The revolt was suppressed in five days.

Numerous executions and arrests followed, as did further oppression of the Irish people as the British Crown tried to stamp out the embers of the independence movement.

2. BLOODY SUNDAY

There were actually two "Bloody Sundays," both the direct result of rebel behavior. One rebellion was violent and one peaceful on the Irish side, but the British slaughtered savagely at both.

The first took place November 21, 1920, in Dublin, when the Black and Tans opened fire on a crowd at a football match, killing twelve in retaliation for the IRA's assassination of thirteen British intelligence officers.

The second was on January 30, 1972, when British commandoes killed thirteen unarmed demonstrators who were taking part in a banned protest march against internment of political prisoners without trial. An inquiry by the Crown found the soldiers innocent of cold-blooded murder, though the surviving unarmed protesters were inclined to disagree.

3. REBELLION OF 1798

The revolutionary fervor as fomented by the successful rebellions in the American colonies and on the streets of Paris, reached the Emerald Isle with less than successful results. A summer of uprising (with some assistance from France) resulted in numerous rebellions around Dublin that were quickly stamped out by the superiority in number and supply of the British forces and the early arrests of most of the leaders. More than thirty thousand died as a direct result of what turned out to be a futile rebellion.

4. THE UPRISING OF 1641

Following the resettlement and reapportionment of all Irish lands (85 percent of which went to lackeys of the Crown), the Irish resentment of their dispossession resulted in the Uprising of 1641, when the Irish natives took up arms against the invading Protestants, supposedly slaughtering more than two thousand newly arrived settlers from Britain.

5. CURRAGH MUTINY

In March 1914, fifty-seven British officers, including General Sir Hubert Gough, declared they would resign rather than enforce home rule against Ulster unionist oppositionists. The commander-in-chief of the British forces in Ireland caved in to their wishes, resulting in a major embarrassment for the British army and the British Secretary of War.

6. THE MISSION OF THE *CATALPA*

The Fremantle Six (Martin Hogan, James Wilson, Thomas Hassett, Michael Harrington, Thomas Darragh, and Robert Cranston) were British soldiers who took the Fenian oath and were subsequently tried for treason and transported to Fremantle Gaol in Western Australia in 1866.

After eight years of internment they managed to escape to the coast, where the *Catalpa*, an American whaler under the command of George Anthony, was waiting for them, ready to battle the elements and the British navy to carry these political prisoners to freedom. They succeeded, and as a result, Captain Anthony never returned to international waters again, always fearing reprisal from her majesty's navy.

7. THE HUNGER STRIKE OF 1981

Robert "Bobby" Sands of Belfast, a member of the Provisional IRA imprisoned in the H Block of Long Kesh prison, led a revolt to reestablish political status to IRA internees. An early attempt at protest through the so-called dirty protest (no bathing, and smearing of excrement on the walls) proved unsuccessful, resulting in the adoption of a more extreme method of protest—a hunger strike.

For sixty days in 1981, Sands and nine others refused nourishment (unto death by starvation) while the unbending Thatcher regime refused to restore their political privileges. As a result Sands became a posthumous icon of Irish patriotism.

8. THE FLIGHT OF THE EARLS

On September 4, 1607, the Earl of Tyrone, the Earl of Tyrconnell, and other leaders of the Ulster rebellion left Ireland rather than being arrested by the incoming British forces. The Earls eventually accepted exile in Rome, never bowing to the Anglican invaders.

9. EMMET'S UPRISING

In July 1803, Robert Emmet and a band of fellow rebels tried to seize Dublin Castle in a surprise attack, only to have their main objective aborted due to a premature off-site powder explosion that tipped off the authorities. The lord chief justice and several other targeted individuals were killed, and Emmet and his men were soon captured and executed.

10. THE KILDARE REVOLT

In 1534, "Silken Thomas" Fitzgerald (so named because of his fashion sense) decided to take advantage of the distractions the King of England was experiencing due to his excommunication problem, by leading a revolt to seize Dublin Castle . . . only to have the Tudors strengthen their hold on the surrounding areas to prevent any recurrence of such an outbreak.

Dublin Castle, object of many revolts.

Irish Warriors Fighting off the Shores of the Emerald Isle

Not all valiant sons of Ireland confined their service to the home front or the wars for Irish independence. Many served the Crown in the farthest reaches of the empire or even far-off powers such as the United States or Argentina as the great Diaspora made Irish bravery known throughout the world.

1. JOHN BARRY (1745-1803)

Born on the Emerald Isle, Barry immigrated to the American colonies as a youth, where he gained employment as a trader and shipmaster. With the coming of the war for independence he commanded the *Lexington*, credited with the capture of a British tender, *HMS Edward*, the first taking of a British ship by a commissioned American vessel. His stature as a naval hero of the revolution was second only to that of John Paul Jones.

2. HERBERT KITCHENER (1850-1916)

Military governor of the Eastern Sudan and commander-in-chief of the Egyptian army, Kitchener was charged by the Crown with the reconquest of the Sudan. He also served as chief of staff to Lord Roberts during the Boer War, and later was appointed commander of British forces in India.

Though he was retired from the military, he served as secretary of state for war during the World War I until he was killed when a ship that was bearing him on a diplomatic mission to Russia struck a German mine and sank.

3. ARTHUR WELLESLEY (1769-1852)

Better known as the Duke of Wellington, Wellesley entered the British Army in 1887 and gained distinction during the peninsular campaigns of the wars with France. He was awarded his dukedom after Napoleon's penultimate defeat and was the architect of Napoleon's final defeat at Waterloo in 1815.

4. CHAIM HERZOG (1918-1997)

Herzog was born on the Emerald Isle and immigrated to Palestine in 1935, where he served valiantly with the Jewish Haganah fighters, the British Army, and the Israeli military.

He eventually was elected president of Israel and served from 1983 to 1993.

5. THOMAS MEAGHER (1823-1867)

A leader of the Young Ireland movement, Meagher escaped to the United States after having been deported to Tasmania. In America he fought with the 69th

Regiment in the Civil War and helped to organize New York's Irish brigade. He finished out his military service under the command of General William Tecumseh Sherman.

6. HAROLD ALEXANDER (1891-1969)

Serving with the Irish Guards in World War I, Alexander rose to the rank of major-general by the outbreak of World War II, during which he was appointed commander-in-chief for the Middle East and then for North Africa. From there he was appointed head of Allied forces in Italy from 1943 to 1944 and eventually was promoted to Supreme Allied Commander in the Mediterranean theater for the duration of the war.

7. EYRE COOTE (1726-1783)

Born in Ash Hill, County Limerick, Coote joined the army at a very early age in hopes of seeking his fortune away from the Emerald Isle. After approximately ten years of service in Scotland, he was promoted to captain and transferred to India, where he had a distinguished military career. His victories against the French at Pondicherry and the rebel sultan of Mysore, Hyder Ali, secured the Crown's control of India in the eighteenth century.

8. CHARLES WILLIAM DE LA POER BERESFORD (1846-1919)

The son of the fourth Marquis of Waterford, Beresford enlisted in the queen's navy at the age of thirteen and earned his first command by 1882, having distinguished himself at the bombardment of Alexandria. He also served in the Nile expedition in 1884, but was later sidetracked by a less successful career in politics.

9. JOHN NICHOLSON (1821-1857)

A valiant son of the Emerald Isle, Nicholson was a fierce and brave warrior who wasn't terribly lucky. During the Afghan Wars he aided in the defense of Ghazni but was ultimately captured and imprisoned at Kabul. Eventually liberated he was later promoted to brigadier general in 1857 only to face the Indian Mutiny of 1857, where, though he defeated resistance in Punjab, he was eventually slain during the storming of Delhi.

10. WILLIAM BROWN (1777-1857)

Born in County Mayo, Brown moved to South America in 1811 to become a government-sanctioned privateer during the war with Spain. Later arrested for piracy, Brown had his commission reactivated during the war with Brazil, where he was eventually given full control of the local navy, distinguishing his command at the Battle of Juncal by securing victory against overwhelming odds.

After a brief stint as governor of Buenos Aires, he returned to his naval command in the campaign against Uruguay.

IRA Guerrilla Objectives

As with any paramilitary organization, the IRA has a strict way of doing things—pragmatic and effective. At all times the goal must be kept in sight, and any short-term gain must be accomplished in accord with the long-term objective.

Below are ten of the IRA's objectives, stated clearly and simply.

1. RECRUITING

Recruit volunteers from the population of the territory of operation.

2. COMMITTEES

Use civil political committees among the people to agitate against the oppressors, leading a campaign of passive and active resistance to the enemy occupation.

3. GUERRILLA AGENTS

Have guerrilla agents collect information among the civilian population.

4. PART-TIMERS

Use part-time guerrillas who will maintain their occupations in the civilian population, yet be available for active service when called up as reserves.

5. BUILD A RAPPORT

Build a rapport between the guerillas and the civilians so the people see the guerillas as their protectors in response to enemy oppression.

6. STAND UP

Provide the people with the tenacity to stand up to the enemy by showing them that the struggle is worthwhile and necessary.

7. PUBLIC OPINION

Get world public opinion behind the just fight through many voices rather a single spokesperson.

8. UNDERMINE ENEMY MORALE

Undermine the enemy's morale and propaganda by exposing his methods and by constant emphasis on the unjustness of his cause.

9. SPIRITUAL MAINSPRING

Be the spiritual mainspring of those actively engaged in the national movement so they understand the need to destroy the enemy and his power forever.

10. NEW MEMBERS

Recruit new members for guerillas and keep them supplied and organized with access to immediate transportation.

Societies and Gangs

Sometimes it's hard to tell the political parties from strong street gangs, social clubs from militant cells, and charitable organizations from organized oppressors.

In the Catholic-Protestant struggle in Irish history nothing can be taken for granted, not even the virtuous intentions of an outlawed gang or the terrorist ambitions of a church charity.

In Ireland, where what would normally be a simple parade is actually a slap in the face to all free Irishman, and a splinter cell is a street-level dispenser of justice, there's never any guarantee of safety in numbers.

1. THE ANCIENT ORDER OF HIBERNIANS

This fraternal society of Irish-American Catholics was founded in New York in 1836 to support Irish immigrants and the homeland whose citizens were being dispersed by the Irish Diaspora. It became politically radicalized later in the century through its support of such revolutionary groups as the Fenians.

Though the Order is still in existence today, it is primarily a network for Catholic charitable services, business networking, and the organization of such social events as annual St. Patrick's Day parades.

2. THE ORANGEMEN

This was the name for members of the exclusively Protestant and unionist Orange Order named after the Protestant hero king, William of Orange, who defeated the Catholic King James in the late 1690s and secured the Crown for the Protestants and thus dominion over all of Britain.

The group survived largely as a social order until the 1880s, when it became a spearhead for the Protestant landlords opposing home rule. The Orangemen's yearly parades are the equivalent of the Ku Klux Klan's rallies in the old South.

3. THE PEEP O'DAY BOYS

The Peep o'Day Boys, a Protestant secret society started in the 1780s, were hell-bent on preserving Protestant privilege and driving the Catholics off their land. The name was derived from the fact that they would usually show up at dawn to burn the farms and further intimidate Catholic families.

4. THE IRISH REPUBLICAN ARMY (IRA)

This militant Irish nationalist organization was founded in 1919 by Michael Collins as the paramilitary wing of Sinn Fein, whose aim was to create a united Irish socialist republic (including Ulster). During the 1919–1921 War of Irish Independence the IRA used guerrilla—some might even say terrorist—tactics to pressure the Crown to the political bargaining table.

In 1969 the army officially split between the "officials" and the "provisionals," giving in to the factionalism that had been tearing them apart for years over the issue of the ends really justifying the means.

5. SINN FEIN

Pronounced "shin fain," which in Irish means "ourselves alone," Sinn Fein is the political wing of the republican movement.

Arthur Griffith founded Sinn Fein in 1905, Eamon de Valera became its president in 1917, and the party won a majority of seats in the 1918 election, which allowed its members to convene a secessionist parliament in Dublin. Wracked by factionalism, the party faded from prominence in the late twenties only to return to the limelight under Gerry Adams after "the Troubles" and during the negotiations of the eighties and the nineties.

6. THE UNKNOWNS

Inspired by the secret squads of the early days of the IRA under Michael Collins, the Unknowns were secret intelligence cells set up by Gerry Adams with a limited chain of command to act on behalf of the Belfast Brigade in the early seventies. The cells, which were small—with three to four members, self-sustaining, and independent of the rest of the Belfast IRA, were set up to combat the betrayals, turncoats, spies, collaborators, and informants that the Crown was using to weaken the army from within.

7. THE CUMANN NA MBAN

Pronounced "cuman naman," the Cumann na mBan is the women's wing of the IRA. Founded in 1913 at the same time as the Irish Volunteers, it worked closely with the factions of militant republicanism and was declared an illegal organization in Northern Ireland in 1922 and in the Irish Free State in 1931.

8. TARTAN GANGS

Teenage loyalist gangs in Belfast were set up in response to the 1971 IRA seduction, abduction, and murder of three Scots soldiers. The gangs were egged on by the Reverend Ian Paisley, who led an impromptu memorial service for the soldiers stressing their ethnic loyalties.

9. THE YOUNG HOOLIGANS

Loosely organized street gangs of late 1960s Derry that bedeviled the police, pelting them with stones and gasoline bombs in the name of civil disobedience. Many of these young men eventually moved up within the IRA and Sinn Fein.

10. THE YOUNG TURKS

These more radical/dedicated young elements of the Belfast brigade (not coincidently, also the acolytes of Gerry Adams) were rounded up in the early seventies in hopes of skewing the brigade away from Adams and more toward a more political, or in their view, peaceful, settlement with the Crown. The belief was that the removal of the young hotheads from the mix would defuse the situation, which turned out to be an almost fatal miscalculation and inspired even more unrest.

Cutthroats and Killers

Ireland has given birth to numerous cutthroats and murderers in the course of its eminent history; many of them, however, decided to ply their trade elsewhere without necessarily despoiling the soil of the Emerald Isle. Still others practiced their butchery at home, literally.

1. BURKE AND HARE

William Burke and William Hare were Ulster born and bred men who sought their fortune in the halls of learning at Edinburgh's finest medical schools. They were not doctors, nor were they teachers. One might say they were independent procurement specialists for scarce and indelicate research subjects of a posthumous nature. Or, in simpler terms, they were body-snatching grave robbers who figured out a way to streamline the process by lining up subjects before they reached the grave, and in some cases before they died, a technicality that the pair remedied quickly through an ingenious method of strangulation that did very little damage to their subjects and thus didn't degrade their value to the pair's acquiring clients.

They were arrested after their sixteenth murder. Hare, who cut a deal and testified against Burke—who was executed on the gallows on January 28, 1829—died a penniless pauper thirty years later, never returning to the land of his birth.

The doctors for whom they procured their subjects were never prosecuted and led prosperous lives afterward, nonetheless enriched by the educational supplements provided by the unlucky pair of murderers.

These two fellows have been immortalized in numerous fictional accounts; probably the most famous one is Dylan Thomas's *The Doctor and the Devils*, which was later filmed with Jonathan Pryce and Stephen Rea in the roles of the supply-side murderers.

2. ANNE BONNEY

Born in Kinsale, Ireland, in the late 1690s, Anne Bonney was the daughter of a penniless maid and her married lawyer lover who later ran off together with Bonney to start a plantation in South Carolina, far from Irish law and the spurned wife.

Bonney adapted well to the less-than-civilized life in the colonies and took up with a small-time pirate who eventually introduced her to Calico Jack Rackham. Disguised as a man, Bonney served as part of his crew, pillaging and slaughtering with the best of the bloodthirsty buccaneers.

When Rackham was later arrested, Bonney was saved from execution by her pregnancy. Her last words to her former lover were: "I'm sorry to see you go, Jack, but if you'd have fought like a man you needn't have had to hang like a dog," at which point Bonney mysteriously vanished from all public record.

3. ED BALL

Nineteen-year-old Ed Ball was a dutiful son, living with his fifty-five-year-old mother until a neighbor noticed bloodstains around the Balls' car. The helpful man notified the police, who promptly searched Ball's premises and discovered numerous bloody towels and newspapers.

Ball claimed that his mother had committed suicide by slitting her own throat, and that he had merely carried out her final wishes by giving her a burial at sea. Unfortunately, his statement did not take into account the bloodstained axe police found in his room.

He was found guilty, but also insane, so he was not executed . . . or maybe the courts just took pity on a poor orphan.

4. PATRICK BYRNE

Patrick Byrne was a twenty-seven-year-old Irish laborer who, under intense interrogation, confessed to the murder of twenty-nine-year-old Stephanie Baird. Baird's body was discovered while the police were investigating an attack on a certain Margaret Brown on December 23, 1959; in the course of their reconnaissance they discovered Baird's beheaded body, followed by the head carefully set atop a bed with the note, "This is the thing I thought would never come."

An autopsy revealed that before the beheading, Baird had been mutilated, molested, and strangled . . . though not necessarily in that order. Byrne was convicted of the crime in March 1960 and sentenced to life imprisonment.

5. DR. PHILIP CROSS

Dr. Philip Cross, a retired army surgeon, lived with his family (wife of eighteen years and six children) in Dripsey. At a certain point a young governess was hired to help out with the children. Cross became overtly smitten with her, resulting in her eventually leaving his employ so they might consummate their ongoing affair more easily.

Early in May 1887, Mrs. Cross began to complain of a stomach malady, which her husband tried to treat but to no avail. Within a month she died of a nonspecific heart ailment. Now needing help with the children given the death of his spouse, Cross reemployed the governess, who promptly moved back in with him and the children. They married in secret two weeks later.

The police became slightly suspicious and exhumed the body of Mrs. Cross only to discover 3.2 grains of arsenic and a modicum of strychnine still in her system. Needless to say, there was no trace of heart disease.

Cross was tried in December 1887 and executed the following January for his ingenious plot to avoid a disadvantageous divorce.

6. IAIN HAY GORDON

On the morning of November 12, 1952, nineteen-year-old Belfast lass Patricia Curran left home for University, never to return again. Her body was discovered horribly mutilated as if she had been shot by a scatter gun (the coroner later concluded that she had actually been stabbed over thirty-five times in rapid succession).

The manhunt for the merciless killer led investigators to the nearby Royal Air Force airbase, where suspicion soon fell on Iain Hay Gordon, who had been acting suspiciously and had known Curran's brother.

Under interrogation Gordon broke down and confessed, claiming he had become overwhelmed with passion for the young girl and had lost control. He was found guilty, but insane as well, so he was incarcerated instead of executed. The verdict was later called into question and overturned.

7. GERARD TOAL

In 1927, Gerard Toal was employed as handyman/chauffeur, along with Mary Callan, in the household of an Irish priest by the name of Father Mckeown.

On May 27, Mary and her bicycle disappeared, never to be seen alive again. Though Toal was initially detained under suspicion since he and Mary had never gotten along, he was nonetheless eventually released due to lack of concrete evidence. Wishing to put the matter behind him, Toal expressed his intention to migrate to Canada for a new beginning, only to have his departure fatally delayed when he was picked up under suspicion of thievery in a nearby town. A new search of his old domicile and workplace turned up parts of Mary's bicycle and burnt remnants of her clothes. A thorough search of a nearby quarry uncovered her badly decomposed body.

Toal was charged with murder and hanged in Dublin on August 29, 1928.

8. KATE WEBSTER

Born Catherine Lawler in County Wexford in 1849, Kate Webster started her criminal career at an early age with numerous counts of petty theft. She eventually resettled in Liverpool, where her efforts in thievery led to her arrest and imprisonment for four years.

Upon release she journeyed to London and accepted a position as a housekeeper in Notting Hill and later made a nice living cleaning out the richer homes of the neighborhood, which eventually earned her several additional prison stints.

In January 1879 she entered the employ of a Mrs. Julia Martha Thomas as a housekeeper/companion. The two got along swimmingly until the beginning of March, the second of the month to be precise, when, in a fit of pique, Webster killed her new friend and employer, first throwing her down the stairs, and then choking her. She then dismembered the body with knife and razor, disposing of the parts in a particularly ghoulish manner, including boiling the remnants, the scent of which gave her away to the neighbors and, soon thereafter, the authorities.

She was tried in January, and, after deliberating for less than two hours, the jury found her guilty. Webster was executed by hanging on the morning of July 29, the perfect example of the efficiency of British crime and punishment when it came to Irish-born felons.

9. WILLIAM BURKE KIRWAN

Commonly referred to as the Ireland's Eye murderer, William Burke Kirwan, an artist of 11 Merrion Street, Dublin, lived with his wife of twelve years, Sara Marie Luisa Kirwan. To all apparent observers, they were the perfect example of wedded bliss.

Summering not far from the island of Ireland's Eye in 1852, Kirwan painted and his wife sunned herself, making the most of their holiday until the coming of fall, when Mrs. Kirwan was found drowned and mutilated on the island.

Kirwan held her funeral, buried her, and then took up with a woman down the block with whom he had been having an affair for several years (he had also fathered seven children by her). Public outcry resulted in his being arrested and charged with murdering his wife.

A sensational trial ensued, filled with innuendo, secret concealed weapons (a sword cane), and numerous bits of contradictory medical testimony, and Kirwan was found guilty and imprisoned.

Kirwan claimed his innocence to the very end. Adultery yes, lack of propriety maybe . . . but murder in such a crude manner? It just wouldn't have been artistic enough.

10. OLIVER CROMWELL

Last but certainly not least is Oliver Cromwell. Although he spent less than ten months in Ireland (August 1649 to May 1650), the Lord Protector's whirlwind military campaign and long-standing political program continued to cause the shedding of blood of the Irish people for years on end.

As a result, the phrase, "the curse of Cromwell be on you," became a favorite invective. It is ironic his most famous portrayal on screen was by an Irishman, Richard Harris, in *Cromwell.*

The Heights of Irish Absurdity

Absurdity is drastically different from humor, and the cavalcade of Irish history and culture are filled with examples of it. It usually involves the sort of disclosures that make you shake your head in disbelief and grin in incredulity.

Sometimes they make you laugh out loud. Sometimes they make you cry. Either way, a point is always made . . . even when that point is neither logical nor just, as has been the lot of the Irish people for almost their entire existence.

1. *A MODEST PROPOSAL* BY JONATHAN SWIFT

Dean Swift's notoriously satiric essay, published in 1729, proposed a solution to the problem of the ongoing famine in Ireland: harvesting the offspring of the poor to feed the masses. Many were outraged by his satiric wit; even more were outraged because they took him seriously.

2. *WAITING FOR GODOT* BY SAMUEL BECKETT

Legendary pioneer playwright of the theater of the absurd, Beckett wrote *En attendant Godot/Waiting for Godot*, composed of two acts during which a pair of itinerants waits for the eponymous Godot, who never shows up. The play is considered to be the modern archetype for theater of expectation in which the audience is led to believe something is going to happen that never does, so playgoers leave with a feeling of disappointment and emptiness (which was the author's intention all along). Talk about bait and switch!

3. *THE CRYING GAME* BY NEIL JORDAN

Is there anyone left who doesn't know the secret of *The Crying Game*? Given the maguffin in Jordan's previous film, *Mona Lisa*, shouldn't discerning cinema fans have seen it coming? In the end those who waited too long to see it had the surprise ruined for them when the Academy Award nominations were revealed to include Jaye Davidson in the Supporting *Actor* category.

But isn't it wonderfully absurd that this 1992 award-winning film can be simply boiled down to "IRA gunman is redeemed by the love of a good woman who turns out to be a man."

4. PUBLICATION OF *ULYSSES* BY JAMES JOYCE

Considered by many to be the seminal modern Irish novel, *Ulysses* depicts a single day in Dublin as experienced by a Jewish advertisement canvasser and a student philosopher in a stream of conscious narrative that mirrors Homer's epic poem, *The Odyssey*. The book was published in 1922 to coincide with Joyce's fortieth birthday; the place of publication, however, was Paris due to scandalous charges of obscenity that banned the book in both the United States and the United Kingdom (and, therefore, Ireland) until 1932 and 1936, respectively.

One might say that this is almost as absurd as, for example, filming a classic western in Italy.

5. ST. PATRICK

Setting aside the curious faerie tale of how he alleged-ly cast out all of the snakes from Ireland, St. Patrick's lock on most popular Irish saint is all the more absurd since he wasn't even born in Ireland. The fact that his claim to fame lies in the success of his mission to bring Christianity to Ireland becomes even more problemat-ic given the role that religion, specifically the schism in Christian sects, has played in the ongoing crucible of pain and oppression that has tortured the Irish for so many years.

St. Patrick

6. *LORD OF THE DANCE*

Michael Flatley, who led the resurgence in popularity of Irish step dancing in *Riverdance* and his own creation, *Lord of the Dance*, was actually born not in Ireland, but in Chicago, Illinois. He was also a noted flautist and a Golden Gloves championship boxer, and when it comes right down to it, he may be a great dancer, but he's an even better self-promoter.

7. THE IRISH INVASION OF CANADA

In June 1866 the American Irish Republican Brotherhood (IRB), also known as the Fenians, invaded Canada in hopes of exerting pressure on the Crown to grant independence to their long-oppressed homeland. Indeed, the Crown recognized the error of its ways and almost as a direct result of these actions granted recognition of dominion to its disputed possession. Unfortunately for the IRB, however, that disputed possession turned out to be Canada.

8. THE "X" CASE

This was one of the most infamous court cases in recent Irish judicial history. In 1992 a fourteen-year-old rape victim was planning to go to England for an abortion when her father inquired of authorities whether "the evidence of the pregnancy" should be retained after the abortion for use in prosecuting the rapist. This led to an overzealous attorney general asking immediately for an injunction preventing the girl from leaving Ireland (where abortion was illegal) for the next nine months in an effort to thwart the desired procedure.

The Supreme Court intervened on her behalf, and the injunction was lifted while she was still in the early stages of her pregnancy.

9. THE ASSASSINATION OF MOUNTBATTEN

On August 1979 Lord Louis Mountbatten, the seventy-nine-year-old cousin of the queen, noted war hero, and perhaps the best-known and popular member of the extended royal family, was killed by a remote-controlled bomb while vacationing off Mullaghmore, County Sligo.

To say that his assassination was a public relations nightmare for the IRA was an understatement. Moreover, it led to even tougher security measures and more invasive crackdowns by agents of the Crown . . . all the more absurd because Mountbatten was also probably the most sympathetic toward Ireland of all of the royal family.

10. . . . BUT WHERE'S GERRY?

In 1998 David Trimble of the Ulster Unionists and John Hume of the Social Democratic and Labour Party were notified that they had been awarded the Nobel Peace Prize for their part in the Good Friday accords. Contrary to the Nobel committee's assessment, the accords were not a bilateral agreement that allowed power sharing but rather a trilateral one. The third party involved was Sinn Fein, and its lead negotiator, Gerry Adams, was more responsible for the peace than either of the other two clean-cut politicians.

Once again a good and pure of heart Irishman was left out in the cold while others took credit for his accomplishments.

Irish Stereotypes

An image doesn't have to be true or accurate to be prevalent. At some point a characterization occurs that strikes a chord with its audience, and "poof," a stereotype is born, ready to be repeated until its validity is no longer questioned and then eventually falls out of favor (which usually has nothing to do with being proven wrong).

1. IRISH SINGING WAITER

Probably best typified by the hard-drinking, merry/melancholic father in Betty Smith's *A Tree Grows in Brooklyn*, the tippling Irish tenor (for some reason never a baritone or bass) who squanders his vocal gift for the false warmth and admiration of the drink is a common bit of fifth business in all things Irish. Sometimes his occupation changes to bartender, but never his vocal range.

2. LONG-SUFFERING AND FRUGAL WIFE OF THE ABOVE

Again the primary source is probably Betty Smith's childhood tale, but later incarnations have become mindful of the co-dependent nature of the role as in Frank McCourt's *Angela's Ashes*, where making ends meet by any means necessary does not always solve the problems at hand.

3. OLD IRISH PRIEST

Barry Fitzgerald's leprechaun-like performances notwithstanding, these men of the cloth were as hard hitting as their pugilist counterparts in the ring. Stern and wise and wielding a ruler like a shillelagh, whether they be Diocesan or Irish Christian brothers, these scions of St. Patrick always knew how to dispense priestly advice while still packing a wallop for use on miscreants and other wayward youths.

4. IRISH COP ON THE BEAT

These products of the immigrant patronage system, Irish cop and fireman stereotypes have their basis in real-life New York from the Boss Tweed era onward. Such jobs were easily obtained without a college (or in some cases a high school) degree, and Hollywood latched onto the New York experience. Sooner than you say Charles MacArthur–Damon Runyon–Joseph Kesselring, films were filled with cops named Murphy and Brophy whose brogues were as thick as a pint of Guinness.

These men on the beat knew everyone's name, and in the days before corruption as defined by Internal Affairs, they were always willing to partake of a piece of baking or an off-duty nip at the corner bar.

5. IRISH BOOTLEGGER

For every cop on the beat, there was a Prohibition-era Irish bootlegger making bathtub gin in his apartment or running a very discreet speakeasy that might be raided periodically but never put out of business. Such activity never seemed to be deemed criminal activity, and after Prohibition, it seemed like everyone just went legit.

6. TOUGH IRISH POLITICAL BOSS

Back in the days when presidents were chosen in smoke-filled rooms by union bosses and independent businessmen (rather than by law school–educated political operatives, corporate CEOs, and yahoo-like thugs from Texas), it was the Tough Irish Political Boss who called the shots.

Best typified in *The Last Hurrah*, these were hard-drinking, smoking party honchos (usually either union bosses or judges or both) who decided in advance whom the rank and file of the party would get the chance to vote for in the final election . . . and in doing so guarantee jobs and or sweet deals for anyone who had earned them through donations of cash. Come to think of it, if you just discount the lack of Irish accents, maybe not much has really changed.

7. THE IRISH REPUBLICAN ARMY GUNMAN WITH A HEART OF GOLD

Long before Fergus in *The Crying Game* or Brad Pitt in *The Devil's Own*, as well as the era when the IRA was looked on as a terrorist organization (under guidelines that would apply equally to America's Sons of Liberty, I believe), there was a public image of the IRA gunman with the heart of gold. Actors like Jimmy Cagney and Victor McLaglen played them as regular-guy heroes. Even Donald Sutherland's Devlin in *The Eagle has Landed* is hard to hate, despite the fact that he's working for the Nazis.

Maybe it was when factions of the group started dealing heroin or allying themselves with anarchists that the golden-boy image began to fade. Most are true freedom fighters; some are opportunistic thugs.

8. HARD-HITTING, ROLLING PIN-WIELDING IRISH BATTLEAXE OF A WIFE

Far from the long-suffering co-dependent of stereotype two above, this formidable female doesn't take any guff from anyone, let alone the man whom she has sworn to love, honor, and obey.

Whether she's played by Marjorie Main or Rita Shaw, this Emerald Isle Amazon is always ready to put her man in his place with a sharp tongue and a kitchen implement of choice, whether he be her husband, son, or soon-to-be son-in-law. Even collegial colleens can become tough old broads when the conditions are right.

9. *ABIE'S IRISH ROSE*

Was there ever a social epidemic where multitudes of male Jews found themselves attracted to Catholic colleens of the Emerald Isle? I'm sure it may have happened once or twice a generation, but surely Italians, Russians, Greeks, etc., also intermarried without becoming the basis for a hit Broadway play and a short-lived TV series.

Then again, maybe it was just one of those made-up situations, sort of the *Big Fat* [fill in the blank] *Wedding* of its era. Odder couples occur all the time, and given the beauty of Irish women, who can blame anyone for falling in love with one?

10. THE JFK-LIKE PRESIDENT

John F. Kennedy was the first Irish Catholic President of the United States, and since the day he was assassinated, his image has provided the archetype for a multitude of Kennedyesque successors in fact and fiction. All from New England, they are of Irish heritage, a humble but proud heritage. You can always pick them out from a crowd by their full heads of hair and penchant for the good life. The era may have been called Camelot, but the king's reign was pure Irish.

Irish Jokes

Though many classic Irish jokes are really variations on archetypal ethnic (insert here) standards, more than a few are deeply rooted in the Irish tradition, history, and way of thinking that comes from a life exulting in all things Irish, and being damned proud of it.

1. THE PRIEST AND THE BRITISH

There was a certain Catholic priest from Belfast who jumped at every opportunity to rail against the British oppressors of the Emerald Isle. Things got so bad that even after numerous warnings the bishop, who decided that he had to intervene, personally warned the priest that the pulpit wasn't the proper place for casting such aspersions, and that he would be reassigned if he was caught doing it again.

The priest apologized for his previous outbursts and vowed to leave his personal politics in the sacristy from then on.

The following Sunday the priest centered his sermon around the Last Supper, and everything was going along in accordance with the bishop's wishes until he came to the part of the betrayal. The priest narrated, "and then our Lord Jesus told his apostles that one of them would betray Him, and they were all shocked, and rushed to proclaim their allegiance to Him."

"Surely not I, Lord" said Peter.

"Nor I," said James.

"Nor I," said John.

"Nor I," intoned all of the others, until it came to Judas Iscariot, who said, "Blimey guv'na, by the queen you don't mean me!"

2. WHAT TYPE OF WOMAN DO YOU THINK I AM?

A certain apocryphal story has been attributed to George Bernard Shaw: it seems that Shaw was at a party discussing his most recent work, the play, *Mrs. Warren's Profession*. The conversation eventually came around to the morality of prostitution. It is alleged that Shaw turned to one of the societal dames in attendance and asked her, hypothetically, if she would go to bed with him for fifty quid. She quickly replied, "Of course not!"

Shaw then asked, hypothetically, if she would go to bed with him for a thousand quid. The lady chuckled and replied that she would definitely have to consider that offer.

Shaw responded, "What about five quid?"

The lady was insulted. "Mr. Shaw!" she protested. "What type of woman do you think I am?"

Shaw replied, "I believe we have already settled that matter. Now we are merely haggling over the price."

3. **HORSE SENSE**

Seamus was doing his summer constitutional when he came across his friend, Paddy, who was up to his neck in a peat bog.

"Will you go fetch some help?" Paddy implored. "Before I sink any lower, I mean."

Now Seamus was a strapping fellow, and he knew Paddy was slight of build, so he decided to help extricate his friend on his own. After several attempts at lifting his friend by the armpits to no avail, while working up quite the manly sweat, Seamus was puzzled.

"I don't understand this," Seamus mused. "I should be able to lift you three times over."

Paddy was equally puzzled, but then offered, "Maybe this time I should take me feet out of the stirrups."

4. **A FAMILY THAT DRINKS TOGETHER**

An Irishman walks into bar in Manhattan and orders three shots of Irish whiskey, which he downs in rapid succession. He then explains to the bartender, "I made a pledge to my two brothers that we would always drink together, even when we're apart. So this one was for Seamus, and this one was for Danny, and this one was for me."

The Irishman returned several times and repeated the ritual each time.

Then one day, he arrived and changed his order, asking only for two shots, instead of the three.

The bartender complied and told him that this time it was on the house. The Irishman nodded and downed the two shots. The bartender then asked which of his brothers had passed on, Seamus or Danny.

"Neither," the Irishman replied, "but I'm the only one of us three who's quit drinking."

5. **A GOOD EDUCATION**

There was a certain demanding Boston grand dame who always imported her maids from Ireland. Into her employ came a pretty young lass, wide-eyed and fresh off the boat, whose quality of work fell below the grand dame's expectations. The mistress decided to upbraid her.

"Siobhan," for that was the lass's name, "see here!" the mistress testily instructed. "I can write my name in the dust on the piano."

Siobhan replied with a twinkle in her eye: "Sure en you can! Ain't education a grand thing?"

6. **BLUE LAWS**

An American tourist decided he wanted to do some skydiving outside of Dublin, so one Sunday a Protestant friend of his took him up in his plane, and out he went, only to discover that the parachute refused to engage.

Lucky for him he landed in a very soft tree, and with the exception of being black and blue from head to toe, he was relatively unscathed.

Once he had managed to climb down, two locals ran up to him to offer assistance and ask what had happened.

"I was skydiving," the tourist replied, and my parachute didn't open."

The locals shook their heads and chuckled.

"You should have checked with one of us beforehand," one replied. "Nothing opens in these parts on Sunday."

7. **DIPLOMACY**

What's Irish diplomacy? The ability to tell a man to go to hell in such a way that he will look forward to the trip.

8. **IRISH MOTHERS**

How do we know that Christ was Irish? At thirty-three he still lived at home with his mother who he thought was a virgin and who treated him like the one true son of God.

9. **WHISKEY HANDICAP**

Why did God invent whiskey? To put the Irish on an equal footing with everyone else (or: To keep the Irish from ruling the world).

10. **A WARNING**

What is black and blue and found floating upside down in the Irish Sea? Someone who tells one too many unfunny Irish jokes.

Museums, Libraries, and Research Centers

Just as the Irish maintained the repositories of Western civilization during the Dark Ages, the Emerald Isle still preserves its past in several notable collections that are available for scholars and tourists alike to educate themselves in the glories and wonders of all things Irish. If this volume has inspired you to further your education in all things Irish, you can do well by availing yourself of the following resources.

1. NATIONAL MUSEUM OF IRELAND

Split between two buildings—one at Kildare and Merrion Streets, the other at the Collins Barracks at Benburb Street—this collection contains arts and artifacts of Irish culture dating back 2000 BCE, as well as such historic artifacts as Wolfe Tone's pocketbook and articles from both the Battle of the Boyne and the sinking of the *Lusitania* to provide a quasi-complete overview of the entire course of Irish history.

2. NATIONAL ARCHIVES

Located at 8 Bishop Street in Dublin, these archives contain the largest variety of genealogical sources on the Emerald Isle, including health and school records, parish registers, land titles, wills, grants, etc., as well as the police papers of the Royal Irish Constabulary.

3. TRINITY COLLEGE LIBRARY

Built in 1732, the library is on the Trinity College campus, just across the O'Connell Bridge on the south side of the River Liffey in Dublin. It was modeled after the library of Trinity College at Cambridge, England, designed by Sir Christopher Wren. Among its precious holdings on display is *The Book of Kells* (each day a page is carefully turned to allow a new view for visitors who are clearly instructed to "keep your hands off!").

4. NATIONAL LIBRARY OF IRELAND

Located on Kildare Street in Dublin, the Library has a very large manuscript collection, sixty-five thousand catalogues containing more than 750,000 individual items and 750,000 volumes in its printed books section. Like Trinity College Library it is one of Ireland's official copyright repositories. The building itself, built in 1810, is also known as the Portobello Barracks. Its exhibit materials now comprise the Irish Defence Force museum.

5. FREE STATE ARMY RECORDS

Located at the Cathal Brugha Barracks, this collection includes the Free State's military archives, among them an early army census from 1922. It is perhaps the most complete collection of documents and other archival material relating to the Rising and the war for independence

6. BELFAST CENTRAL LIBRARY

Located on Royal Avenue in Dublin Castle, the BCL houses the former collection of Sir Alfred Chester Beatty, including cuneiform clay tablets, Coptic papyri, and vellum manuscripts in Hebrew, Sanskrit, Syriac, and Samaritan. There are also three thousand Arabic manuscripts as well as Indian, Siamese, and Tibetan documents.

7. LINEN HALL LIBRARY

Located at 17 Donegal Square in North Belfast, this archival collection, established in 1788, contains one of the largest collections in the world of books dealing with the linen trade, along with archival materials from 1791 forward and the meteorological records of Belfast from 1796 to 1906. Of historical note, its first official librarian (Thomas Russell) was hanged for treason in 1803.

8. FRANCISCAN LIBRARY

Located on Seafield Road in Killiney, Dublin, this was indeed one of the places where "the Irish saved civilization." It has an authoritative collection of Gaelic manuscripts from the eleventh to the twentieth centuries and includes the *Annals of the Four Masters* up to 1169 CE.

9. DUBLIN WRITERS MUSEUM

Located at 18 Parnell Square, North Dublin, this exhibition and repository of the works and workers of Irish letters and literature of the past three hundred years is located in a renovated eighteenth-century mansion. It was first opened in 1991.

10. DUBLIN CIVIC MUSEUM

Located at 58 South William Street in Dublin, in a building that was once the Civic Assembly House, the museum houses exhibits tracing the history of the city from Viking times to the present in terms of both its geographical development and its cultural and mercantile evolution.

Bibliography

The Book of Irish Weirdness. New York: Quality Paperback Book Club, 1995.

Handbook for Volunteers of the Irish Republican Army. Boulder, Colo.: Paladin Press, 1985.

1798-1998—Irish Songs, Tunes, and Speech of Rebellion, Resistance & Reconstruction. London: Retro, 1998.

Adams, Gerry. *Cage Eleven.* New York: Sheridan Square, 1993.

———. *Falls Memories: A Belfast Life.* Niwot, Colo.: Roberts Rinehart, 1994.

Asala, Joanne. *Irish Saints & Sinners.* New York: Sterling Publishing Company, 1995

Bennett, Richard. *The Black and Tans.* New York: MetroBooks, 2002.

Bolger, Dermot. *The Vintage Book of Contemporary Irish Fiction.* New York: Vintage Books, 1995.

Boyer, Paul. *The Oxford Companion to American History.* Oxford: Oxford University Press, 2001.

Brady, Ciaran. *The Hutchison Encyclopedia of Ireland.* Oxford: Helicon Publishing, 2000.

Cahill, Tom. *How the Irish Saved Civilization.* New York: Doubleday Books, 1995.

Coughlin, Patrick. *Irish Saints.* London: Mercier Press, 1999.

Connolly, S. J. (ed.). *The Oxford Companion to Irish History.* Oxford: Oxford University Press, 2002.

Cooghan, Tim Pat. *Where ever Green Is Worn: The Story of the Irish Diaspora.* New York: Palgrave Publishing, 2001.

Corcoran, J. Aeneas. *Irish Ghosts.* New Lanark, Scotland: Geddes & Grosset, 2002

Cordingly, David. *Under the Black Flag*. New York: Random House, 1995.

Craddock, Jim. *VideoHound's Golden Movie Retriever 2001*. New York: Visible Ink Press, 2001.

Cronin, Mike, and Daryl Adair. *The Wearing of the Green—A History of St. Patrick's Day*. London: Routledge, 2002.

Cross, Tom P., and Clark Harris Slover (eds.). *Ancient Irish Tales*. New York: Barnes & Noble Books, 1996.

Cullen, Bill. *It's a Long Way from Penny Apples*. New York: Tom Doherty Associates, 2003.

Dangerfield, George. *The Damnable Question—A History of Anglo-Irish Relations*. New York: Barnes & Noble Books, 1976.

Drabble, Margaret (ed.). *The Oxford Companion to English Literature*, 6th ed. Oxford: Oxford University Press, 2000.

Ellis, Peter Berresford. *Erin's Blood Royal—The Gaelic Noble Dynasties of Ireland*. New York: Palgrave, 2002.

Ellman, Richard. *James Joyce* (rev. ed.). Oxford: Oxford University Press, 1983.

———. *Oscar Wilde*. New York: Alfred A. Knopf, 1988.

English, T. J. *The Westies—Inside Hell's Kitchen Irish Mob*. New York: Putnam, 1990.

Haining, Peter (ed.). *Great Irish Stories of Childhood*. New York: Barnes & Noble Books, 1997.

Holmes, Richard (ed.). *The Oxford Companion to Military History*. Oxford: Oxford University Press, 2001.

Hunt, Lindsay. *Fodor's Exploring Ireland*, 4th ed. New York: Fodor's Travel Publications, 2001.

Igoe, Vivien. *A Literary Guide to Dublin*. London: Methuen, 1999.

Kearns, Kevin C. *Dublin Tenement Life—An Oral History*. New York: Penguin Books, 2000.

Kipling, Rudyard. *The Irish Guards in the Great War*. New York: Sarpedon Publishers, 1997.

Lehr, Dick, and Gerard O'Neill. *Black Mass—The True Story of an Unholy Alliance Between the FBI and the Irish Mob*. New York: Public Affairs, 2000.

Lydon, James. *The Making of Ireland—From Ancient Times to the Present*. London: Routledge, 1998.

Maddox, Brenda. *Yeats's Ghosts: The Secret Life of W. B. Yeats*. New York: HarperCollins Publishers, 1999.

Massie, Sonja. *The Complete Idiot's Guide to Irish History and Culture*. New York: Alpha Books, 1999.

Matthews, John (ed.). *From the Isles of Dream*. Edinburgh: Floris Books, 1993.

McAnally, D. R., Jr. *Irish Wonders*. New York: Grammercy Books, 1996.

McCullough, David Willis. *Wars of the Irish Kings*. New York: Crown Publishers, 2000.

Moloney, Ed. *The Secret History of the IRA*. New York: W. W. Norton & Company, 2002.

O'Brien, Sinead (with David G. Allen). *Ireland for Dummies*. New York: Hungry Minds, 2001.

Power, Patrick C., and Sean Duffy. *Timetables of Irish History*. London: Worth Press, 2001.

Reid, Gerard (ed.). *Great Irish Voices—Over 400 Years of Irish Oratory*. Dublin: Irish Academic Press, 1999.

Shaw, Antony. *Portable Ireland*. London: Running Press, 2002.

Stevens, Peter F. *The Voyage of the Catalpa*. New York: Carroll & Graff Publishers, 2002.

Toibin, Colm. *The Penguin Book of Irish Fiction*. New York: Viking Press, 1999.

Toolis, Kevin. *Rebel Hearts—Journeys Within the IRA's Soul*. New York: St. Martin's Press, 1995.

Williams, Paul. *The Evil Empire*. New York: Forge Books, 2004.

———. *The General*. New York: Forge Books, 2003.

Yeats, William Butler. *Irish Fairy and Folk Tales*. New York: Barnes & Noble Books, 1993.

Index

Numbers is *italics* refer to pages with illustrations

271